TELL ME WHY #1

BY ARKADY LEOKUM

ILLUSTRATIONS BY HOWARD BENDER

GROSSET & DUNLAP • New York

CONTENTS

Chapter 3
The Human Body

Chapter 4
How Other Creatures Live

Chapter 5

How Things Are Made

TELL ME WHY

#1

CHAPTER 1
OUR WORLD

HOW BIG IS THE UNIVERSE?

It is impossible for the human mind to conceive a true picture of the size of the universe. We not only don't know how big it is, but it is hard for us even to imagine how big it might be.

If we start from the earth and move out, we'll see why this is so. The earth is part of the solar system, but a very tiny part of it. The solar system consists of the sun, the planets that revolve around it, the asteroids, which are tiny planets, and the meteors.

Now, this whole solar system of ours is only a tiny part of another, much bigger system called "a galaxy." A galaxy is made up of many millions of stars, many of which may be much larger than our sun, and they may have solar systems of their own.

So the stars we see in our galaxy, which we call "the Milky Way," are all suns. They are all so far away that distances are measured in light years instead of in miles. Light travels about 6,000,000,000,000 miles in a year. The bright star nearest to the earth is Alpha Centauri. Do you know how far away it is? 25,000,000,000,000 miles!

But we're still talking only about our own galaxy. This is believed to be about 100,000 light years in width. This means 100,000 times 6,000,000,000,000 miles! And our galaxy is only a tiny part of a still larger system.

There are probably millions of galaxies out beyond the Milky Way.

And perhaps all these galaxies put together are still only a part of some larger system!

So you see why it is impossible for us to have an idea of the size of the universe. Incidentally, it is believed by scientists that the universe is expanding. This means that every few billion years two galaxies will find themselves twice as far apart as they were before!

WHY IS THE SOLAR SYSTEM THE WAY IT IS?

As far as we know, there is no reason why the solar system is arranged exactly as it is. It might have been arranged differently, just as there are other solar systems in the universe arranged differently. This has to do with the way it originated. But man has discovered certain laws of nature that seem to keep the solar system in its present pattern.

Earth, like the other planets, follows its path, or orbit, around the sun. The period of time that the earth takes to go around the sun is called a year. The other planets have orbits larger or smaller than the earth's.

How this solar system came to be and how the planets came to have the size, location, and orbits they have, astronomers cannot fully explain. But they have two main types of theories. One type of theory suggests that the formation of the planets was a part of the gradual change of the sun from a whirling mass of hot gas to its present size and brilliance. The planets formed as small whirling masses in the giant gas and dust cloud as it turned.

Another group of theories is based on the idea that at some time there was a near-collision between the sun and another star passing nearby. Large pieces of the sun were pulled away and began to revolve around the sun at different distances. These are now planets.

No matter which theory is right, the solar system came to be as it now is more or less by chance. Why does it stay this way? Kepler's Laws of Planetary Motion state that all planets travel about the sun in an elliptical (oval) path; that a planet moves faster in its orbit as it nears the sun; and that there is a relation between its distance from the sun and the time it takes to make an orbit. Newton's Law of Gravitation, of which Kepler's three laws were an indispensable part, explained how two objects attract each other. So the solar system remains as it is because certain laws of nature maintain the relationship of the sun and the planets.

WHAT KEEPS THE SUN SHINING?

It may be hard for you to believe, but when you look at the stars that shine at night and the sun that shines by day, you are looking at the same kinds of objects!

The sun is really a star. In fact, it's the nearest star to the earth. Life as we know it depends on the sun. Without the sun's heat, life could not have started on earth. Without sunlight, there would be no green plants, no animals, no human beings.

The sun is 93,000,000 miles from the earth. The volume, or bulk, of the sun is about 1,300,000 times that of the earth! Yet an interesting thing about the sun is that it is not a solid body like the earth.

Here is how we know this: The temperature on the surface of the sun is about 11,000 degrees Fahrenheit. This is hot enough to change any metal or rock into a gas, so the sun must be a globe of gas!

Years ago, scientists believed that the reason the sun shone, or gave off light and heat, was that it was burning. But the sun has been hot for hundreds of millions of years, and nothing could remain burning for that long.

Today scientists believe that the heat of the sun is the result of a process similar to what takes place in an atom bomb. The sun changes matter into energy.

This is different from burning. Burning changes matter from one form to another. But when matter is changed into energy, very little matter is needed to produce a tremendous amount of energy. One ounce of matter could produce enough energy to melt more than a million tons of rock!

So if science is right, the sun keeps shining because it is constantly changing matter into energy. And just one per cent of the sun's mass would provide enough energy to keep it hot for 150 billion years!

WHAT IS THE EARTH MADE OF?

A sort of rough answer to this question would be: The earth is a big ball, or sphere, made mostly of rock. Inside the earth the rock is melted, but the outside cover is hard rock. Less than one-third of the earth's surface is land and more than two-thirds are water.

Now let's consider this in a little more detail. The outside of the earth is a crust of rock about 10 to 30 miles thick. This crust is sometimes called "the lithosphere." The high parts of this crust are the continents, and the low parts of it hold the waters of the oceans and the great inland seas and lakes. All the water on the surface, including the oceans, lakes, rivers, and all the smaller streams, is called "the hydrosphere."

Men have been able to examine only the outermost part of the crust of rock that forms the outside of the earth, which is why it's so hard to know what the earth is like on the inside. In drilling wells and digging mines, it has been found that the deeper the hole is made, the higher the temperature becomes. At two miles below the surface of the earth, the temperature is high enough to boil water.

But scientists have also been able to find out about the inside of the earth from studies of earthquakes. They believe that the temperature does not increase as rapidly deep down as it does in the crust. So they think that at the core or center of the earth the temperature may not be more than 10,000 degrees Fahrenheit. Of course, that's plenty hot—since a temperature of 2,200 degrees would melt rocks!

The crust of the earth has two layers. The upper layer, which makes the continents, is of granite. Under the layer of granite is a thick layer of very hard rock called "basalt." Scientists believe that at the center of the earth is a huge ball of molten iron, with a diameter of about 4,000 miles. Between the central ball and the rocky crust is a shell about 2,000 miles thick called "the mantle." The mantle is probably made of a kind of rock called "olivine."

WHAT IS A CONSTELLATION?

Have you ever looked at the stars and traced out squares, letters, and other familiar figures? In nearly all parts of the world, people of long ago did this and gave names to the group of stars they observed. Such a group is called "a constellation," from the Latin terms meaning "star" (stella) and "together."

The names of the constellations in use today have come down to us from the times of the Romans and from the even more ancient Greeks. What the Greeks knew about the stars came partly from the Babylonians.

The Babylonians named some of their star figures after animals and others after kings, queens, and heroes of their myths. Later, the Greeks

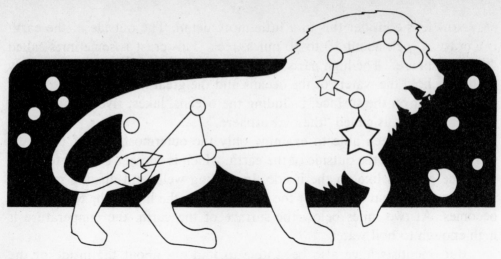

The Constellation Leo

changed many of these Babylonian names to the names of their own heroes such as Hercules, Orion, and Perseus. The Romans made further changes. The same ancient names are still used, but it is not always easy to make out in the sky the figures that suggested them. For example, Aquila is the eagle, Canis Major and Canis Minor are big and little dogs, and Libra is the scales, but the constellations don't look much like these figures to us.

About the year A.D. 150, the famous astronomer Ptolemy listed 48 constellations that were known to him. This list did not cover the entire sky; there were many blank spots. So, in later times, astronomers added constellations to Ptolemy's list. Some of these later constellations are named for scientific instruments, such as the Sextant, the Compasses, and the Microscope. Today, astronomers recognize 88 constellations in the sky.

A constellation is really an area in the sky. This means that every star lies in one constellation or another, just as any city in the United States is in some one state. The boundaries of the constellations used to be very irregular. Many of them had curved lines. But in 1928, astronomers decided to straighten them out so that the outline of any constellation includes only straight lines.

WHAT IS THE MILKY WAY?

There is probably nothing more mysterious and wonderful-looking in the sky than the Milky Way, stretching like a band of jewels from one end of the sky to the other. In ancient times, when people gazed at this spectacle, they were filled with the wonder and beauty of it just as you are. But since they didn't really know what it was, they made up all sorts of strange and beautiful explanations of the Milky Way.

For example, in early Christian times, people thought it was a pathway for the angels, so they could go up to heaven on it. Or they imagined it was an opening in the heavens, so that we here on earth could have a glimpse of the glory that existed beyond.

Knowing the facts about the Milky Way, as we do today, doesn't remove any of the wonder of it. The facts are just as amazing as any "made-up" idea!

Our galaxy is shaped roughly like a watch, round and flat. If you could get above it and look down on it, it would look like an immense watch. But we are inside the galaxy, and when we look up we are looking towards the edge from inside the "watch." So we see that edge curving around us. And since there are millions of stars in it, we see it as the Milky Way.

Did you know that there are at least 3,000,000,000 stars in the galaxy? And here is an idea of its size. It takes eight minutes for light from the sun to reach the earth. For light from the center of the galaxy to reach the sun, it takes about 27,000 years!

The galaxy rotates about its center like a wheel. From our position in it, it takes about 200,000,000 years just to make one revolution!

WHAT IS THE BRIGHTEST STAR?

Have you ever looked up at the sky and tried to find the brightest star?

You may imagine that the number of stars you can see is countless. But the most that can be seen without a telescope are about 6,000 stars, and one-quarter of them are too far south to be seen in North America.

Ever since the days of the Greek astronomers, 2,000 years ago, the stars have been divided into classes according to their magnitude or brightness. Until the invention of the telescope, only six magnitudes, or degrees of brightness, were recognized. Stars of the first magnitude are the brightest, and stars of the sixth magnitude the faintest. Stars fainter than the sixth magnitude cannot be seen without a telescope. Today, stars can be photographed with modern telescopes down to the 21st magnitude.

A star of any given magnitude is about two and a half times fainter than a star of the magnitude above it. There are 22 stars of the first magnitude, the brightest stars, and the brightest star of all is Sirius, which has a magnitude of −1.6. This makes Sirius over 1,000 times brighter than the faintest star that can be seen with the naked eye.

The lower we go down in magnitude, the more stars there are in that class. Thus, there are 22 stars of the 1st magnitude and about 1,000,000,000 stars of the 20th magnitude.

WHAT ARE FALLING STARS?

For thousands of years men have looked up at "falling stars" and wondered what they were and where they come from. At one time it was believed that they came from other worlds.

Today we know that they are not "stars" at all. We call them "meteors." They are small, solid bodies which travel through space, and which may also pass through the earth's atmosphere.

When meteors come within our atmosphere, we can see them because they leave a fiery train of light. This is caused by the heat made by the friction, or rubbing, of air upon their surfaces.

Strangely enough, most individual meteor particles are quite small, about the size of a pinhead. Occasional meteors weigh many tons. Most meteors are destroyed entirely by heat as they pass through the earth's atmosphere. Only the larger meteor fragments ever reach the earth. Scientists believe that thousands of meteors fall to earth each day and night, but since most of the earth's surface is covered by water, they usually fall into oceans and lakes.

Meteors may appear in the sky singly and travel in practically any direction. But meteors usually occur in swarms of thousands. As the earth travels in its path around the sun, it may come close to such swarms of of meteors, they become fiery hot upon contact with the upper layers of the atmosphere, and we see a "meteoric shower."

Where do meteors come from? Astronomers now believe that the periodic swarms of meteors are the broken fragments of comets. When comets break up, the millions of fragments continue to move through space as a meteor swarm or stream. The swarms move in regular orbits, or paths, through space. One such swarm crosses the earth's path every 33 years.

When a piece of meteor reaches the earth, it is called "a meteorite." It has fallen to the earth because gravity has pulled it down. Far back in

Roman times, in 467 B.C., a meteorite fell to the earth and its fall was considered such an important event that it was recorded by Roman historians!

WHAT IS A COMET?

At one time, the appearance of a comet caused people to tremble with fear. They believed that comets were evil omens foretelling plagues, wars, and death.

Today, we have a pretty good idea of what comets are, though we still don't have all the answers about them. When a comet first appears, it is seen as a tiny point of light, though it may be thousands of miles in diameter.

This point of light is "the head," or nucleus, of the comet. Scientists think it is probably made of a great swarm of bits of solid matter, combined with gases. Where this matter originally came from is what is still a mystery.

As the comet approaches the sun, a tail usually appears behind it. The tail consists of very thin gases and fine particles of matter that are shot off from the comet's nucleus when it comes under the influence of the sun. Surrounding the nucleus of the comet is a third portion, known as "the coma." It is a glowing cloud of matter that sometimes reaches a diameter of 150,000 miles, or even more.

Comet tails are very different in shape and size. Some are short and stubby. Others are long and slender. They are usually at least 5,000,000 miles in length. Sometimes they are almost 100,000,000 miles long! Some comets have no tails at all.

As the tail grows, the comet gains in speed because it is nearing the sun, moving toward it head first. Then a curious thing happens. When the comet goes away from the sun, it goes tail first with the head following. This is because the pressure of light from the sun drives off the very small particles from the comet's head to form its tail, always in a direction away from the sun.

As a result, when the comet goes away from the sun, its tail must go first. During its journey away from the sun, the comet gradually slows down and then disappears from sight. Comets may remain out of sight for many years, but most of them reappear eventually. Comets make trip after trip around the sun, but they may require a long time to make a single revolution. Halley's Comet, for example, takes about 75 years to make its trip around the sun.

At present, astronomers have listed almost 1,000 comets, but there must be several hundred thousand comets in our solar system which remain unseen!

WHY IS THE OCEAN SALTY?

Every now and then, we come across a fact about our earth which mystifies us and for which no answer has yet been found. Such a fact is the existence of salt in the oceans. How did it get there?

The answer is we simply don't know how the salt got into the ocean! We do know, of course, that salt is water-soluble, and so passes into the oceans with rain water. The salt of the earth's surface is constantly being dissolved and is passing into the ocean.

But we don't know whether this can account for the huge quantity of salt that is found in oceans. If all the oceans were dried up, enough salt would be left to build a wall 180 miles high and a mile thick. Such a wall would reach once around the world at the Equator! Or put another way, the rock salt obtained if all the oceans dried up would have a bulk about 15 times as much as the entire continent of Europe!

The common salt which we all use is produced from sea water or the water of salt lakes, from salt springs, and from deposits of rock salt. The concentration of salt in sea water ranges from about three per cent to three-and-one-half per cent. Enclosed seas, such as the Mediterranean and the

Red Sea, contain more salt in the water than open seas. The Dead Sea, which covers an area of about 340 square miles, contains about 11,600,000,000 tons of salt!

On the average, a gallon of sea water contains about a quarter of a pound of salt. The beds of rock salt that are formed in various parts of the world were all originally formed by the evaporation of sea water millions of years ago. Since it is necessary for about nine-tenths of the volume of sea water to evaporate for rock salt to be formed, it is believed that the thick rock-salt beds that are found were deposited in what used to be partly enclosed seas. These evaporated faster than fresh water entered them, and the rock-salt deposits were thus formed.

Most commercial salt is obtained from rock salt. The usual method is to drill wells down to the salt beds. Pure water is pumped down through a pipe. The water dissolves the salt and it is forced through another pipe up to the surface.

WHICH OCEAN IS THE DEEPEST?

In many ways, the oceans still remain a great mystery to us. We don't even know how old the oceans are. It seems certain that in the first stages of the earth's growth no oceans existed.

Today, man is exploring the bottoms of the oceans to learn more about them. Covering the floor of the ocean to a depth of 12,000 feet is a soft, oozy mud. It is made up of the limy skeltons of tiny sea animals. The floor of the deep, dark regions of the sea, where the water is more than four miles deep, is covered by a fine, rusty-colored ooze called "red clay." It is made up of tiny parts of skeltons of animals, the coverings of tiny plants, and volcanic ash.

The way the depth of oceans is measured today is by sending down sound waves which are reflected back from the bottom. The depth is found by measuring the time it takes for the sound wave to make the round trip and dividing this time in half.

Based on these measurements, we have a pretty good idea of the average depth of various oceans, and also the deepest point in each one. The ocean which has the greatest average depth is the Pacific Ocean. This is 14,048 feet. Next in average depth is the Indian Ocean which has an average of

13,002. The Atlantic is third with an average depth of 12,880 feet. The Baltic Sea is at the other extreme, with an average depth of only 180 feet!

The single deepest spot so far known is in the Pacific near Guam, with a depth of 35,400 feet. The next deepest spot is in the Atlantic off Puerto Rico where it measures 30,246. Hudson Bay, which is larger than many seas, has its deepest point at only 600 feet!

WHAT CAUSES WAVES IN THE WATER?

If you've ever spent some time near a body of water, then you noticed that on a calm day there are very few waves in the water, and on a windy or stormy day there are many waves.

This, of course, explains what causes waves in the water. It is the wind. A wave is a way in which some form of energy is moved from one place to another. Some sort of force or energy must start a wave, and the wind provides that energy in the water.

When you watch the waves move, one after the other, the water seems to move forward. But if there is a piece of floating wood in the water, it will not move forward as the waves seem to do. It will only bob up and down with the waves. It moves only when the wind or tide moves it.

Then what kind of motion is taking place in a wave? A water wave is mostly the up-and-down movement of water particles. The movement passes on toward the shore, but not the particles of water. For example, if you have a rope you can send a kind of wave along the rope. The up-and-down movement passes along the rope, but not the particles of the rope.

As the bottom of a water wave strikes the ground a short distance from the beach, it slows up because of friction. The top keeps going, and then topples over, and thus forms a "breaker."

The energy that formed the waves loses itself against the shoreline. All you have to do is stand among the waves along a beach and you'll soon find out that they have energy!

In a water wave, the water particles move in a circular path, up and forward, as they are pushed by the wind. Then they move down and back as gravity draws the heaped-up water back to a common level. These up-and-down movements carry the wave along.

The distance from crest to crest of a wave is the wave length, and the low point is called "the trough."

WHAT IS THE GULF STREAM?

The Gulf Stream is an ocean current, the most famous ocean current of all. It is like a river that flows through the sea instead of on land. But the Gulf Stream is so vast that it is larger than all the rivers in the world put together!

The Gulf Stream moves northward along the coast of Eastern United States, across the North Atlantic Ocean, and then to northwest Europe. The Gulf Stream has a clear indigo-blue color and it can be seen clearly where it contrasts with the green and gray waters that it flows through.

The water of the Gulf Stream comes from the movement of the surface waters near the Equator in the Atlantic. This movement or "drift" is westward. So the Gulf Stream starts by moving north of South America and into the Caribbean Sea. It actually becomes what we call the Gulf Stream when it starts moving northward along the east coast of the United States.

Since the Gulf Stream starts in the warm part of the world, it is a current of warm water. And the presence of this huge current of warm water makes amazing differences in the climate of many places!

Here are some curious examples of this: Winds passing over this current in northern Europe (where it is called "the North Atlantic Drift") carry warm air to parts of Norway, Sweden, Denmark, The Netherlands, and Belgium. Result—they get milder winter temperatures than other places just as far north! It also means that ports along the Norwegian coast are ice-free the year round.

Thanks to the Gulf Stream, London and Paris enjoy mild winter climates, though they lie just as far north as southern Labrador, for example, which has bitterly cold winters. The winds that pass over the Gulf Stream are made warm and moist. When these winds become chilled, as they do near Newfoundland, dense fog results. And so we have the famous dangerous fogs of the Grand Banks of Newfoundland.

The Gulf Stream doesn't have as great an effect on the winter climate of North America as on Europe, because the winter winds don't blow over it and then inland, as they do in Europe.

HOW WERE THE MOUNTAINS FORMED?

Because mountains are so big and grand, man thinks of them as unchanging and everlasting. But geologists, the scientists who study mountains, can prove that mountains do change, and that they are not everlasting.

Certain changes in the earth's surface produced the mountains, and they are constantly being destroyed and changed. Boulders are broken from mountainsides by freezing water; soil and rock particles are carried away by rainwash and streams. In time, even the highest mountains are changed to rolling hills or plains.

Geologists divide mountains into four classifications, according to how they were formed. All mountains, however, are the result of violent changes in the earth's surface, most of which happened millions of years ago.

Folded mountains were made of rock layers, squeezed by great pressure into large folds. In many places in such mountains, you can see the rock layers curving up and down in arches and dips, caused by the squeezing and pressure on the earth's surface. The Appalachian Mountains and the Alps of Europe are examples of folded mountains.

In dome mountains, the rock layers were forced up to make great blister-like domes. In many cases, molten lava, coming with great pressure from below the earth's surface, lifted these rock layers. The Black Hills of South Dakota are examples of dome mountains.

Block mountains are the result of breaks, or faults, in the earth's crust. Huge parts of the earth's surface, entire "blocks" of rock, were raised up or tilted at one time. The Sierra Nevada Range of California is a block that is 400 miles long and 80 miles wide!

Volcanic mountains are built of lava, ash, and cinders poured out from within the earth. The usual volcano is cone-shaped with a large hole, or crater, at the top. Among the famous volcanic mountains are Mounts Ranier, Shasta, and Hood in the United States, Fujiyama in Japan, and Vesuvius in Italy.

Many mountain ranges have been formed by more than one of the ways described. In the Rockies are mountains made by folding, faulting, doming, and even erosion of lava!

HOW ARE CAVES FORMED?

Caves have long been linked with the history of man in many interesting ways. We know that late in the Old Stone Age, caves were the winter dwelling place of people who had no other shelter.

But long after man stopped using caves as homes, ancient people

believed many strange things about caves. The Greeks believed caves were the temples of their gods, Zeus, Pan, Dionysus, and Pluto. The Romans thought that caves were the homes of nymphs and sibyls. The ancient Persians and others associated caves with the worship of Mithras, chief of the earth spirits.

Today, huge and beautiful caves all over the world are tourist attractions. Caves are deep hollow places in the rocky sides of hills or cliffs. Large caves are called "caverns."

Caves are formed in many different ways. Many caves have been hollowed out by the constant beating of the sea waves against the rocks. Some caves appear under the surface of the earth. These are usually the old courses of underground streams which have worn away layers of soft rock such as limestone. Others are formed by the volcanic shifting of surface rocks, or by the eruption of hot lava.

The most common type of cave in the United States is that made by the wearing away of thick layers of limestone. This is done by the action of water containing carbon dioxide. In Indiana, Kentucky, and Tennessee, where there are great beds of limestone with an average thickness of 175 feet, such caves are numerous.

Some caves have openings through their roofs, called "sink holes." These formed where the surface water first gathered and seeped down. Some caves have galleries in tiers or rows, one above another. Underground streams wind through some caves, though in many cases after a cave has been formed, the streams that once flowed through it may find a lower level and leave the cave dry.

In many cases, each drop of water that drips from a cave roof contains a bit of lime or other mineral matter. As part of the water evaporates, some of this matter is left behind. It gradually forms a stalactite, shaped like an icicle hanging from the roof. Water dripping from the stalactite to the floor builds up a column called "a stalagmite."

WHAT ARE FOSSILS?

The study of fossils is so important in helping man learn about his own past and that of animals who lived millions of years ago that it has developed into a separate science called "paleontology."

Fossils are not, as some people think, the remains of bodies buried ages ago. Actually, there are three different kinds of fossils. The first is part of the actual body of the organism, which has been preserved from decay, and which appears just as it was originally. But fossils may also be just the cast or mold of the shape of the body, which remains after the body of the plant or animal has been removed. And fossils may merely be the footprints or trails that animals have left as they moved over the soft muds or clays.

When a fossil is found that consists of part of the organism itself, it is usually only the hard parts, such as shells or skeletons, that are preserved. The softer parts are destroyed by decay. Yet, in some cases, even such soft-bodied animals as jellyfish, which are 99 per cent water, have left perfect fossils of themselves in rocks! And certain fossils found encased in ice not only have the skeleton preserved but also the flesh and skin on the bones.

Fossils have nothing to do with size. For instance, the fossils of tiny ants which lived millions of years ago can be found perfectly preserved in amber. The chances for animals being preserved as fossils depend mostly on where they lived. The most numerous of all fossils are water animals because when they die their bodies are quickly covered over by mud and so kept from decaying. Land animals and plants are exposed to the destroying action of the air and weather.

It is chiefly through the study of fossils that we know about animal life as it existed millions and hundreds of millions of years ago. For example, fossils taken from certain rocks tell us that millions of years ago there was an Age of Reptiles, with monsters so huge that they were 80 feet long and weighed 40 tons. These were the dinosaurs. And our entire knowledge about the earliest bird, called "the archaeopteryx," is based on just two fossils of it that have been found!

WHEN DID THE ICE AGE END?

Most people think of the Ice Age as something that happened so long ago that not a sign of it remains. But did you know that geologists say we are just now reaching the end of the Ice Age? And people who live in Greenland are actually still in the Ice Age as far as they're concerned.

About 25,000 years ago, any people who may have been living in central North America saw ice and snow the year round. There was a great wall of ice that stretched from coast to coast, and the ice extended northward without an end. This was the latest Ice Age, and all of Canada, much of the United States, and most of northwestern Europe were covered by a sheet of ice thousands of feet thick.

This didn't mean that it was always icy cold. The temperature was only about 10 degrees lower than it is now in Northern United States. What caused the Ice Age was that the summers were very cool. So there wasn't enough heat during the summer months to melt away the winter's ice and snow. It just continued to pile up until it covered all the northern area.

But the Ice Age really consisted of four periods. During each period the ice formed and advanced, then melted back toward the North Pole. It is believed this happened four times. The cold periods are called "glaciations," and the warm periods are called "interglacial" periods.

It is believed that in North America the first period of ice came about 2,000,000 years ago, the second about 1,250,000 years ago, the third about 500,000 years ago, and the last about 100,000 years ago.

The last Ice Age didn't melt at the same rate everywhere. For example, ice that reached what is now Wisconsin began to melt about 40,000 years ago. But ice that had covered New England melted about 28,000 years ago. And there was ice covering what is now Minnesota until about 15,000 years ago!

In Europe, Germany got from under the ice 17,000 years ago and Sweden remained covered with ice until about 13,000 years ago!

WHY DO WE STILL HAVE GLACIERS TODAY?

The great ice mass that began the Ice Age in North America has been called "a continental glacier; it may have been about 15,000 feet thick in its center. This great glacier probably formed and then melted away at least four times during the Ice Age.

The Ice Age or glacial period that took place in other parts of the world still has not had a chance to melt away! For instance, the big island of Greenland is still covered with a continental glacier, except for a narrow fringe around its edge. In the interior, this glacier often reaches heights of more than 10,000 feet. Antarctica is also covered by a vast continental glacier which is 10,000 to 12,000 feet high in places!

So the reason we still have glaciers in certain parts of the world is that they have not had a chance to melt away since the Ice Age. But most of the glaciers that exist today have been formed in recent times. These glaciers are usually the valley type of glacier.

It starts in a broad, steep-walled valley shaped like a great amphitheatre. Snow is blown into this area or slides in from avalanches from the slopes above. This snow doesn't melt during the summer but gets deeper year by year. Eventually, the increasing pressure from above, together with some melting and refreezing, forces the air out of the lower part of the mass and changes it into solid ice. Further pressure from the weight of ice and snow above eventually squeezes this mass of ice until it begins to creep slowly down the valley. This moving tongue of ice is the valley glacier.

There are more than 1,200 such glaciers in the Alps of Europe! Glaciers are also found in the Pyrenees, Carpathian, and Caucasus Mountains of Europe, and in southern Asia. In southern Alaska, there are tens of thousands of such glaciers, some from 25 to 50 miles long!

WHY DO WE HAVE DIFFERENT SEASONS?

Since earliest times, man has been curious about the changing of the seasons. Why is it warm in summer and cold in winter? Why do the days gradually grow longer in the spring? Why are the nights so long in winter?

We all know the earth revolves around the sun, and at the same time it revolves on its own axis. As it moves around the sun, it's also spinning like a top. Now if the axis of the earth (the line from the North Pole through the South Pole) were at right angles to the path of the earth around the sun, we would have no such thing as different seasons, and all the days of the year would be of equal length.

But the axis of the earth is tilted. The reason for this is that a combination of forces is at work on the earth. One is the pull of the sun, the other is the pull of the moon, the third is the spinning action of the earth itself. The result is that the earth goes around the sun in a tilted position. It keeps that same position all year, so that the earth's axis always points in the same direction, toward the North Star.

This means that during part of the year the North Pole tilts toward the sun and part of the year away from it. Because of this tilt, the direct rays of the sun sometimes fall on the earth north of the Equator, sometimes directly on the Equator, and sometimes south of the Equator. These differences in the way the direct rays of the sun strike the earth cause the different seasons in different parts of the world.

When the Northern Hemisphere is turned toward the sun, the countries north of the Equator have their summer season, and the countries south of the Equator have their winter season. When the direct rays of the sun fall on the Southern Hemisphere, it is their summer and it is winter in the Northern Hemisphere. The longest and shortest days of each year are called "the summer solstice" and "winter solstice."

There are two days in the year when night and day are equal all over the world. They come in the spring and fall, just halfway between the solstices. One is the autumnal equinox, which occurs about September 23, and the other is the spring equinox, which occurs about March 21.

WHAT IS HUMIDITY?

If you put a pitcher of ice water on a table and let it stand a while, what happens? Moisture gathers on the outside of the pitcher. Where does this moisture come from? It comes from the air.

The fact is there is always moisture in the air in the form of water vapor. In the case of the ice pitcher, the vapor condensed on the cold surface of the pitcher and thus became visible. But water vapor in the air is invisible. And the word "humidity" simply means the presence of water vapor in the air. It is found everywhere, even over great deserts.

This means, of course, that we always have humidity, but the humidity is not always the same. We have several ways of expressing the humidity, and two of them are "absolute humidity" and "relative humidity." Let's see what each means.

"Absolute humidity" is the quantity of water vapor in each unit volume of air. There are so many grains per cubic foot of air. But for most practical purposes, this doesn't tell us very much. If you want to know whether you'll feel comfortable or not, the answer "four grains per cubic foot" won't tell you whether the air will feel dry or humid. The more easily moisture from your body can evaporate into the air, the more comfortable you'll be. The evaporative power of the air depends on the temperature, and absolute humidity doesn't indicate anything about the evaporative power of the air.

Relative humidity is expressed as a percentage. "One hundred per cent" stands for air which is saturated or completely filled with water vapor. The higher the temperature, the greater the quantity of water vapor air can hold. Thus, on a hot day, a "90 per cent relative humidity" means an awful lot of moisture in the air—a day that will make you mighty uncomfortable.

WHAT IS FOG?

A fog is a cloud in contact with the ground. There is no basic difference between a fog and a cloud floating high in the atmosphere. When a cloud is near or on the surface of the earth or sea, it is simply called "fog."

The commonest fogs are those seen at night and in the early morning over the lowlands and small bodies of water. They usually are caused by a cold current of air from above striking down upon the warmer surface of the land or water.

In the autumn they are very common, because the air is cooling faster day by day than the land or the water. On still nights after dark, thin layers of fog often form close to the ground in low places. As the earth cools at night, the lower air gets cooler. Where this cooler air meets the moist warmer air just above, fog forms.

As a general rule, city fogs are much thicker than country fogs. City air is full of dust and soot that mingle with tiny particles of water to form a thicker blanket.

Off the coast of Newfoundland, which is one of the foggiest parts of the world, fogs are formed by the passage of damp, warm air over the cold water flowing south from the Arctic Circle. The chill of the water condenses the moisture of the air into tiny drops of water. These drops are not big enough to fall as rain. They remain in the air as fog.

San Francisco fogs are formed in the opposite way. There a cool morning breeze blows over warm sand dunes, and if rain has moistened the sand the night before, a thick fog bank of evaporated moisture forms.

The reason fogs often seem denser than clouds is that the droplets are smaller in a fog. A large number of small drops absorb more light than a smaller number of large drops (as found in clouds), and thus it seems denser to us.

WHAT IS DEW?

You would imagine that dew is a very simple phenomenon of nature, easily understood and explained. Yet strangely enough, exactly what dew is has long been misunderstood, and whole books have been written on the subject!

Since the days of Aristotle until about 200 years ago, it was believed that dew "fell," somewhat like rain. But dew doesn't fall at all! The most familiar form of dew, seen on the leaves of plants, is now known not to be all dew! So you see, there have been many wrong ideas about dew.

In order to understand what dew is, we have to understand something about the air around us. All air holds a certain amount of moisture. Warm air can hold much more water vapor than cold air. When the air comes in contact with a cool surface, some of that air becomes condensed and the moisture in it is deposited on the surface in tiny drops. This is dew.

The temperature of the cool surface, however, has to drop below a certain point before dew will form. That point is called "the dew point." For example, if you place water in a glass or a polished metal container, dew may not collect on the surface. If you place some ice in the water, dew may still not collect until the surface of the glass or container is brought down to a certain point.

How does dew form in nature? First, there has to be moisture-laden warm air. This air must come into contact with a cool surface. Dew doesn't form on the ground or sidewalk, because it still remains warm after having been heated by the sun. But it may form on grasses or plants which have become cool.

Then why did we say that the dew seen on plants is really not dew? The reason is that while a small part of the moisture seen on plants in the morning is dew, most of it—and in some cases all of it— has really come from the plant itself! The moisture comes out through the pores of the leaves. It is a continuation of the plant's irrigation process for supplying the leaves with water from the soil. The action starts in the daytime, so that the surface of the leaf should be able to withstand the hot sun, and it simply continues into the night.

In some places in the world, enough dew is deposited every night for it to be collected in dew ponds and used as a water supply for cattle!

WHY DOES THUNDER FOLLOW LIGHTNING?

Lightning and thunder must have been among the first things about nature that mystified and frightened primitive man. When he saw the jagged tones of lightning in the sky and heard the claps and rumbles of thunder, he believed the gods were angry and that the lightning and thunder were a way of punishing man.

To understand what lightning and thunder actually are, we must recall a fact we know about electricity. We know that things become electrically charged—either positively or negatively. A positive charge has a great attraction for a negative one.

As the charges become greater, this attraction becomes stronger. A point is finally reached where the strain of being kept apart becomes too great for the charges Whatever resistance holds them apart, such as air, glass, or other insulating substance, is overcome or "broken down." A discharge takes place to relieve the strain and make the two bodies electrically equal.

This is just what happens in the case of lightning. A cloud containing countless drops of moisture may become oppositely charged with respect to another cloud or the earth. When the electrical pressure between the two becomes great enough to break down the insulation of air between them, a lightning flash occurs. The discharge follows the path which offers the least resistance. That's why lightning often zigzags.

The ability of air to conduct electricity varies with its temperature, density, and moisture. Dry air is a pretty good insulator, but very moist air is a fair conductor of electricity. That's why lightning often stops when the rain begins falling. The moist air forms a conductor along which a charge of electricity may travel quietly and unseen.

What about thunder? When there is a discharge of electricity, it causes the air around it to expand rapidly and then to contract. Currents of air rush about as this expansion and contraction take place. The violent collisions of these currents of air are what we hear as thunder. The reason thunder rolls and rumbles when it is far away is that the sound waves are reflected back and forth from cloud to cloud.

Since light travels at about 186,284 miles per second and sound at about 1,100 feet per second through air, we always see the flash first and then hear the thunder later.

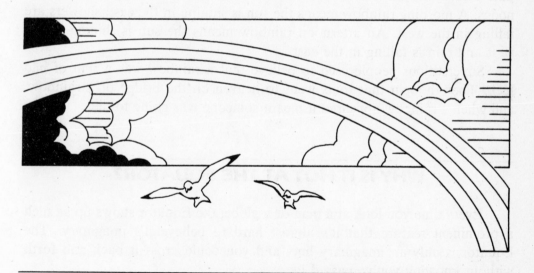

WHAT IS A RAINBOW?

A rainbow is one of the most beautiful sights in nature, and man has long wondered what makes it happen. Even Aristotle, the great Greek philosopher, tried to explain the rainbow. He thought it was a reflection of the sun's rays by the rain, and he was wrong!

Sunlight, or ordinary white light, is really a mixture of all the colors. You've probably seen what happens when light strikes the beveled edge of a mirror, or a soap bubble. The white light is broken up into different colors. We see red, orange, yellow, green, blue, and violet.

An object that can break up light in this way is called "a prism." The colors that emerge form a band of stripes, each color grading into the one next to it. This band is called "a spectrum."

A rainbow is simply a great curved spectrum, or band of colors, caused by the breaking-up of light which has passed through raindrops. The raindrops act as prisms.

A rainbow is seen only during showers, when rain is falling and the sun is shining at the same time. You have to be in the middle, the sun behind you, the rain in front of you, or you can't see a rainbow! The sun shines over your shoulder into the raindrops, which break up the light into a spectrum, or band of colors. The sun, your eyes, and the center of the arc of the rainbow must all be in a straight line!

If the sun is too high in the sky, it's impossible to make such a straight line. That's why rainbows are seen only in the early morning or late afternoons. A morning rainbow means the sun is shining in the east, showers are falling in the west. An afternoon rainbow means the sun is shining in the west and rain is falling in the east.

Superstitious people used to believe that a rainbow was a sign of bad luck. They thought that souls went to heaven on the bridge of a rainbow, and when a rainbow appeared it meant someone was going to die!

WHY IS IT HOT AT THE EQUATOR?

Every time you look at a map or a globe, the Equator shows up as such a prominent feature that it's almost hard to believe it's imaginary. The Equator is only an imaginary line, and you could cross it back and forth without knowing you've passed it.

This may explain why sailors like to remind themselves that they're "crossing the line," as they call it, by making quite a ceremony of it. The word "Equator" comes from a Latin word meaning "to equalize." And this is what the Equator does. It divides the earth into the Northern and Southern Hemispheres. It is the imaginary line that encircles the earth midway between the North and South Poles.

Imaginary lines, encircling the earth parallel to the Equator are called "parallels." The Equator is the zero line, and lines above and below it measure latitude for locating points on the earth's surface.

The earth, as you know, is also divided on maps into regions. Starting at the top or north, we have the Arctic Region, the North Temperate Region, the Tropical Region, the South Temperate Region, and the Antarctic Region.

The Tropical Region, or the Equatorial Region, extends beyond the Equator to 23½ degrees north latitude and to 23½ degrees south latitude. Within this region, the rays of the sun come down vertically, and therefore it is always hot here.

Let's see why this is so: The earth, as you know, has its axis tilted to its path around the sun. The Equator, therefore, is tilted to this path, too, and that tilt is exactly 23½ degrees. Because of this tilt, as the earth goes around the sun, the direct rays from it sometimes fall on the earth north of the Equator, sometimes directly on the Equator, and sometimes south of the Equator. The sun, however, cannot be directly overhead more than 23½ degrees from the Equator.

This explains why the Equatorial Region is the only place on earth where the sun's rays come down vertically. You can understand why, since this happens the year round, it's always pretty hot near the Equator!

WHAT IS SMOKE?

Smoke is the result of incomplete combustion of certain fuels. This means that if most of our common fuels were able to burn completely, we would have no smoke!

Most fuels consist of carbon, hydrogen, oxygen, nitrogen, a little sulphur, and perhaps some mineral ash. Now, if these fuels would burn completely, the final product would be carbon dioxide, water vapor, and free nitrogen, all of which are harmless. If sulphur is present, small quantities of sulphur dioxide are also given off, and when this comes in contact with air and moisture, it becomes a corrosive acid.

For complete combustion, a fuel must have enough air for full oxidation at a high temperature. These conditions are difficult to obtain, especially with solid fuels, and the result is smoke. Anthracite and coke can be burned without producing smoke because they have no volatile matter.

But bituminous coals decompose at rather low temperatures so that gases and tarry matter are freed; they combine with dust and ash and produce smoke.

The air in any city is full of suspended solid particles, but not all of this is smoke. It may contain dust, vegetable matter, and other materials. All of these gradually settle under the force of gravity. In small towns or suburbs, probably about 75 to 100 tons of these deposits settle down per square mile during a year. In a big industrial city, the deposits may be 10 times as great!

Smoke can do a great deal of harm. It damages health, property, and vegetation. In big industrial towns, it lowers the intensity of the sunshine, especially the ultraviolet rays which are essential to health.

If the wind didn't spread the smoke, big industrial towns would probably have fog every day. In fact, where smoky fog occurs, it often happens that the death rate goes up from lung and heart diseases.

The effect of smoke on vegetation is especially harmful. It interferes with the "breathing" of plants and screens off needed sunlight. Quite often, the acid in the smoke destroys plants directly!

Today, many cities are waging active campaigns to cut down on smoke or to prevent it from doing damage.

WHAT IS SMOG?

Between December 4th and 9th, 1952, in the City of London, about 4,000 people died as a result of exposure to smog! What is smog and why is it so dangerous?

In some cities the combination of different industrial gases released into the air makes up a kind of fog we call "smog." It makes people cough when they breathe it. If certain fumes and fine particles are present in the smog, it can become poisonous.

Now, dust is present in the air at all times. Dust is tiny particles of solid matter that can be carried in suspension by air. Dust may come from soil blowing, ocean spray, volcanic activity, forest fires, the exhaust from automobiles, and from industrial combustion processes. The latter is what you see pouring out of factory chimneys.

The amount of dust in the air is almost unbelievable. It is estimated that over the United States about 43,000,000 tons of dust settle every year!

Of this amount, about 31,000,000 tons are from natural sources. That leaves about 12,000,000 tons of dust that are the result of human activities!

Naturally, the amount of dust is greatest in big industrial cities. For example, here is roughly how much dust falls per square mile each month in some of our big cities: Detroit—72 tons; New York—69 tons; Chicago—61 tons; Pittsburgh—46 tons; and Los Angeles—33 tons. In a section of the city where there are many industrial buildings, it might be as much as 200 tons per square mile each month.

This is such an important health problem that many cities are carrying on intensive campaigns to reduce the amount of industrial dust in the air. Dust-producing machinery is built with hoods to keep the dust down. Ventilation systems, blower fans, and electrical devices that cause the dust to settle are also used. In some cases, wet drilling is done and water sprays are used, too. But the problem of dangerous dust in the air—or "smog"—has not yet been licked.

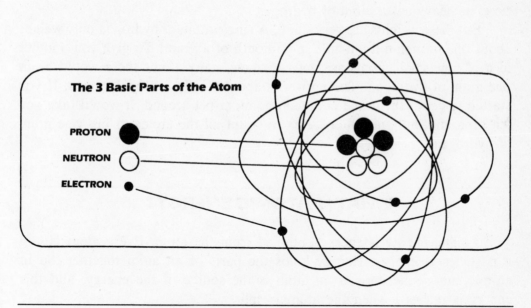

The 3 Basic Parts of the Atom

PROTON

NEUTRON

ELECTRON

HOW BIG IS AN ATOM?

Let us begin by saying that anything we know about the atom today might be changed tomorrow. Science is constantly learning new things about the atom as atom-smashing machines are built.

Oddly enough, the word "atom" comes from the Greek and means "not divisible.'' The ancient Greeks thought an atom to be the smallest possible particle of any substance.

Yet today we have found more than 20 different particles in the core of the atom! Scientists believe the atom is made of electrons, protons, neutrons, positrons, neutrinos, mesons, and hyperons. Electrons are particles that carry a tiny negative charge of electricity. The proton, about 1,836 times as heavy as the electron, carries a positive charge of electricity. The neutron, still heavier, carries no electric charge at all. The positron, about the size of the electron, carries a positive charge. The neutrino, about one two-thousandth the size of the electron, has no charge. Mesons may be either positively or negatively charged. Hyperons are larger than protons.

How all these particles or charges are held together to make up the atom is still not known to us. But these atoms make up the elements and they differ from each other. One way they differ is by weight, and thus elements are classified according to atomic weights. For example, hydrogen is "1" on this table and iron is "55." This means that an atom of iron is 55 times as heavy as an atom of hydrogen.

But these weights are very small. A single atom of hydrogen only weighs about one million-million-million-millionth of a gram! To give you another idea of how small atoms are, let's see how many atoms there would be in one gram of hydrogen. The answer is about 6 followed by 23 zeros. If you started to count them and counted one atom per second, it would take you ten thousand million million years to count all the atoms in just one gram of hydrogen!

WHAT IS ATOMIC ENERGY?

Atomic energy is energy obtained from the atom. Every atom has in it particles of energy. Energy holds the parts of an atom together. So in atomic energy the core of an atom is the source of the energy, and this energy is released when the atom is split.

But there are actually two ways of obtaining energy with atoms. One is called "fusion" and one is called "fission." When fusion takes place, two atoms are made to form one single atom. The fusion of atoms results in the release of a tremendous amount of energy in the form of heat. Most of the energy given off from the sun comes from fusion taking place in the sun. This is one form of atomic energy.

Another form of atomic energy comes from the fission process. Fission happens when one atom splits into two. This is done by bombarding or hitting atoms with atomic particles such as neutrons (one of the particles that make up the atom).

An atom doesn't split every time it is bombarded by neutrons. In fact, most atoms cannot be made to split. But uranium and plutonium atoms will split under proper conditions.

One form of uranium called "U-235" (it is known as an "isotope" of uranium), breaks into two fragments when it is struck with neutrons. And do you know how much energy this gives off? One pound of U-235 gives much more than 1,000,000 times as much energy as could be obtained by burning one pound of coal! A tiny pebble of uranium could run an ocean liner or an airplane or even a generator.

WHAT IS RADIUM?

Radium is a radioactive element. Let us see what "radioactive" means.

Elements are made up of atoms. Most atoms are stable, which means they do not change from year to year. But a few of the heaviest atoms break down and change into other kinds. This breakdown or decay is called "radioactivity."

Each radioactive element decays or disintegrates by giving off rays at a certain rate. This rate cannot be hurried or slowed by any known method. Some change rapidly, others slowly, but in all cases the action cannot be controlled by man.

In the case of radium, this decay would go on and on until the radium would be finally changed into lead. For example, half a gram of radium would change to atoms of lower atomic weight in 1,590 years. After another 1,590 years, half of the remaining radium would change; and so on until it all became lead.

Radium was discovered by Madame Curie and her husband, Pierre Curie. They were refining a ton of pitchblende, which is an ore that contains uranium. They knew the uranium was giving off invisible rays, but they felt there must be some other substance there, too, much more powerful. First they found polonium, another radioactive element, and finally they succeeded in isolating a tiny speck of radium.

Radium gives off three kinds of rays, called *alpha, beta,* and *gamma* rays. *Alpha* rays are fast-moving particles of the gas helium. *Beta* rays are fast-moving electrons. And *gamma* rays are like X-rays but usually more penetrating. Whenever one of these rays is ejected, the parent atom from which it comes changes from one element to another. This change is called "atomic transmutation."

WHAT IS RADIOACTIVITY?

Hardly anyone can grow up in the world today without hearing about—and worrying about—radioactivity. We know that testing of atom bombs creates radioactivity, which is why it is one of the greatest problems facing mankind today. But just what is radioactivity—and why is it harmful to man?

Let's start with the atom. Every kind of atom is constructed somewhat like our solar system. Instead of the sun there is a nucleus, and instead of planets there are electrons revolving around it. The nucleus is made up of one or more positively charged particles.

Radioactivity occurs when something happens to cause the atom to send off one or more particles from its nucleus. At the same time, the atom may send out energy in the form of rays (gamma rays).

Now some elements are naturally radioactive. This means the atoms are constantly discharging particles. When this happens, we say it is "disintegrating." When particles are sent off, the element undergoes a change. In this way, radium—which is naturally radioactive—sends off particles and disintegrates into other elements until it becomes lead.

Scientists have now learned how to produce artificial radioactivity. By bombarding the atoms of certain elements with particles, they could make those atoms begin to disintegrate and thus become radioactive. The bombarded atoms would thus send off energy. That's why these machines are called "atom smashers."

Why is radioactivity dangerous to man? Well, just picture these flying particles coming from the smashed atoms. When these particles strike other atoms, they can cause them to break up, too, and change their chemical character. Now, if these particles strike living cells in the body, they certainly can cause changes there! They can burn and destroy the skin, destroy red blood cells, and cause changes in other cells.

So while radioactivity can be useful to man in many ways, it can also be dangerous and destructive.

WHAT ARE X-RAYS?

X-rays were discovered in Germany in 1895 by Wilhelm Roentgen, and thus are sometimes called "Roentgen rays."

They are penetrating rays similar to light rays. They differ from light rays in the length of their waves and in their energy. The shortest wave length from an X-ray tube may be one fifteen-thousandth to one-millionth of the wave length of green light. X-rays can pass through materials which light will not pass through because of their very short wave length. The shorter the wave length, the more penetrating the waves become.

X-rays are produced in an X-ray tube. The air is pumped from this tube until less than one hundred-millionth of the original amount is left. In the tube, which is usually made of glass, there are two electrodes. One of these is called "the cathode." This has a negative charge. In it is a coil of tungsten wire which can be heated by an electric current so that electrons are given off. The other electrode is "the target," or "anode."

The electrons travel from the cathode to the target at very great speeds because of the difference between the cathode and the target. They strike

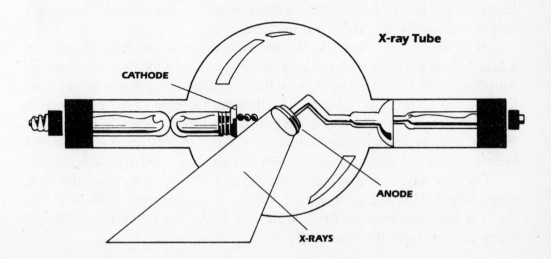

X-ray Tube

CATHODE

ANODE

X-RAYS

the target at speeds that may vary from 60,000 to 175,000 miles per second.

The target is either a block of tungsten or a tungsten wheel, and it stops the electrons suddenly. Most of the energy of these electrons is changed into heat, but some of it becomes X-radiation, and emerges from a window at the bottom as X-rays.

Have you ever wondered how X-ray pictures are taken of bones in your body? The X-ray "picture" is a shadowgraph or shadow picture. X-rays pass through the part of the body being X-rayed and cast shadows on the film. The film is coated with a sensitive emulsion on both sides. After it is exposed, it is developed like ordinary photographic film. The bones and other objects the X-rays do not pass through easily cast denser shadows and so show up as light areas on the film.

Today, X-rays play an important part in medicine, science, and industry, and are one of man's most helpful tools.

WHAT CAUSES A MIRAGE?

Imagine a wanderer in the desert, dying of thirst. He looks off into the distance and sees a vision of a lake of clear water surrounded by trees. He stumbles forward until the vision fades and there is nothing but the hot sand all around him.

The lake he saw in the distance was a mirage. What caused it? A mirage is a trick Nature plays on our eyes because of certain conditions in the atmosphere. First we must understand that we are able to see an object because rays of light are reflected from it to our eyes. Usually, these rays reach our eye in a straight line. So if we look off into the distance, we should only see things that are above our horizon.

Now we come to the tricks the atmosphere plays with rays of light. In a desert, there is a layer of dense air above the ground which acts as a mirror. An object may be out of sight, way below the horizon. But when rays of light from it hit this layer of dense air, they are reflected to our eyes and we see the object as if it were above the horizon and in our sight. We are really "seeing" objects which our eyes cannot see! When the distant sky is reflected by this "mirror" of air, it sometimes looks like a lake, and we have a mirage.

On a hot day, as you approach the top of a hill, you may think the road ahead is wet. This is a mirage, too! What you are seeing is light from the sky that has been bent by the hot air just above the pavement so that it seems to come from the road itself.

Mirages occur at sea, too, with visions of ships sailing across the sky! In these cases, there is cold air near the water and warm air over it. Distant ships, that are beyond the horizon, can be seen because the light waves coming from them are reflected by the layer of warm air and we see the ship in the sky!

One of the most famous mirages in the world takes place in Sicily, across the Strait of Messina. The city of Messina is reflected in the sky, and fairy castles seem to float in the air. The Italian people call it *Fata Morgana,* after Morgan Le Fay, who was supposed to be an evil fairy who caused this mirage.

HOW FAST DOES SOUND TRAVEL?

Every time a sound is made, there is some vibrating object somewhere. Something is moving back and forth rapidly. Sound starts with a vibrating object.

But sound must travel in something. It requires something to carry the sound from its source to the hearer. This is called "a medium." A medium can be practically anything—air, water, objects, even the earth. The Indians used to put their ears to the ground to hear a distant noise!

No medium—no sound. If you create a vacuum, space containing no air or any other substance, sound cannot travel through it. The reason for this is that sound travels in waves. The vibrating objects cause the molecules or particles in the substance next to them to vibrate. Each particle passes on the motion to the particle next to it, and the result is sound waves.

Since the mediums in which sound travels can range from wood to air to water, obviously the sound waves will travel at different speeds. So when we ask how fast does sound travel, we have to ask: In what?

The speed of sound in air is about 1,100 feet per second (750 miles per hour). But this is when the temperature is 32 degrees Fahrenheit. As the temperature rises, the speed of sound rises.

Sound travels much faster in water than in air. When water is at a temperature of 46 degrees Fahrenheit, sound travels through it at about 4,708 feet per second, or 3,210 miles per hour. And in steel, sound travels at about 11,160 miles per hour!

You might imagine that a loud sound would travel faster than a weak sound, but this isn't so. Nor is the speed of sound affected by its pitch (high or low). The speed depends on the medium through which it is traveling.

If you want to try an interesting experiment with sound, clap two stones together when you are standing in the water. Now go under water and clap those two stones together again. You'll be amazed how much better sound travels through water than through air!

WHAT IS THE SOUND BARRIER?

The name "sound barrier" is actually a wrong way to describe a condition that exists when planes travel at certain speeds. A kind of "barrier" was expected when planes reached the speed of sound — but no such barrier developed!

In order to understand this, let's start with a plane traveling at ordinary low-speed flight. As the plane moves forward, the front parts of the plane send out a pressure wave. The pressure wave is caused by the building-up of particles of air as the plane moves forward.

Now this pressure wave goes out ahead of the plane at the speed of sound. It is, therefore, moving faster than the plane itself, which, as we said, is moving at ordinary speed. As this pressure wave rushes ahead of the plane, it causes the air to move smoothly over the wing surfaces of the approaching plane.

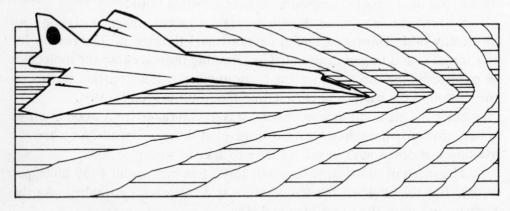

Now let's say the plane is traveling at the speed of sound. The air ahead receives no pressure wave in advance of the plane, since both the plane and the pressure wave are moving forward at the same speed. So the pressure wave builds up in front of the wing.

The result is a shock wave, and this creates great stresses in the wing of the plane. Before planes actually flew at the speed of sound and faster, it was expected that these shock waves and stresses would create a kind of "barrier" for the plane — a "sound barrier." But no such barrier developed, since aeronautical engineers were able to design planes to overcome it.

Incidentally, the loud 'boom" that is heard when a plane passes through the "sound barrier" is caused by the shock wave described above — when the speed of the pressure wave and the speed of the plane are the same.

WHAT IS FIRE?

The scientific name for burning is "combustion." There are many different kinds of combustion, but in most cases a very simple thing has to take place. Oxygen from the air has to combine with some material that can burn.

This reaction produces heat. If the process takes place rapidly, we may see flames or an intense glow or actually feel the combustion, as in an explosion. When wood or paper combine with oxygen, we usually have flames. But we also have combustion in the engines of our automobiles. The gasoline burns with oxygen taken from the air.

In the automobile engine the combustion proceeds so rapidly that we call it an explosion. At the opposite end, we have a kind of combustion that goes on so slowly that we may not notice it for years. For instance, when iron rusts, a slow burning process is actually taking place!

When slow combustion takes place and the heat that results cannot escape into the air, the temperature may reach a point where active burning begins. This is called "spontaneous combustion." Spontaneous combustion might occur in a heap of oily rags left in some closed place. The oil will undergo slow oxidation or burning which results in heat. Since the heat cannot escape, it accumulates. Eventually there will be enough heat to cause the cloth to burst into flames.

Oxygen, which is necessary in combustion, is one of the most common elements in nature. The air which surrounds us contains approximately 21 per cent of oxygen. This oxygen is always ready to enter the combustion process.

However, materials which are "combustible" are as necessary as oxygen for combustion to take place. We call these materials "inflammable." Inflammable materials which are planned to be used for combustion are known as "fuels." For instance, wood, coal, coke, fuel oil, kerosene, and certain gases are common fuels.

During combustion, two atoms of oxygen from the air combine with one atom of carbon from the fuel to form a molecule of a new substance called "carbon dioxide." Did you know that the combustion process which goes on in our body to generate heat and energy creates carbon dioxide which we breathe out?

WHAT IS OXYGEN?

Every now and then you read about something that man "couldn't live without." Well, one thing you can be sure is absolutely necessary to life is oxygen. Without oxygen, a human being cannot live more than a few minutes.

Oxygen is an element, the most plentiful element in the universe. It makes up nearly half of the earth's crust and more than one-fifth of the air. Breathed into the lungs, it is carried by the red blood corpuscles in a constant stream to the body cells. There it burns the food, making the heat needed to keep the human engine going.

Oxygen combines very easily with most elements. When this takes place, we call the process "oxidation." When this oxidation takes place very quickly, we have "combustion." In almost all oxidations, heat is given off. In combustion, the heat is given off so fast that it has no time to be carried away, the temperature rises extremely high, and a flame appears.

So at one end we have combustion, the fast oxidation that produces fire and at the other end we have the kind of oxidation that burns the food in our body and keeps the life process going. But slow oxidations, by the oxygen of the air, are found everywhere. When iron rusts, paint dries, alcohol is changed into vinegar, oxidation is going on.

The air we breathe is a mixture chiefly of nitrogen and oxygen. So we can prepare pure oxygen from the air. It is done by cooling the air to very low temperatures until it becomes liquid. This temperature is more than 300 degrees below zero Fahrenheit. As soon as the liquid air warms up a little above that temperature, it boils. The nitrogen boils off first and oxygen remains. Many a life has been saved by giving people oxygen to make breathing easier when their lungs were weak.

WHAT IS WATER?

When scientists wonder whether there is life on other planets, they often ask this question: "Is there water there?" Life as we know it would be impossible without water.

Water is a tasteless, odorless, colorless compound that makes up a large proportion of all living things. It occurs everywhere in the soil, and exists in varying amounts in the air.

Living things can digest and absorb foods only when these foods are dissolved in water. Living tissue consists chiefly of water. What is water made of? It is a simple compound of two gases: hydrogen, a very light gas; and oxygen, a heavier, active gas.

When hydrogen is burned in oxygen, water is formed. But water does not resemble either of the elements which compose it. It has a set of properties all its own.

Water, like most other matter, exists in three states: a liquid state, which is the common form; a solid, called "ice"; and a gas, called "water vapor." In which one of these forms water shall exist depends ordinarily on the temperature.

At 0 degrees centigrade, or 32 degrees Fahrenheit, water changes from the liquid to the solid state, or freezes. At 100 degrees centigrade, or 212 degrees Fahrenheit, it changes from the liquid to the gaseous state. This change from liquid, visible water to the invisible water gas is called "evaporation."

Thus, if a piece of ice is brought into a warm room, it starts to become liquid or melt. If the room is warm enough, the little puddle of water formed from the melting ice finally disappears. The liquid is changed into water vapor. When water is cooled, it expands just before it reaches the freezing point.

Water as it occurs in nature is never pure in the true sense. It contains dissolved mineral material, dissolved gases, and living organisms.

HOW IS SOIL FORMED?

If the surface of our earth were not covered with soil, man would perish. Without soil, plants could not grow and human beings and other animals would have no food.

Soil is the loose, powdery earth in which plants grow. It is made up of very small pieces of rock and decayed plant and animal materials. The small pieces or particles of rock were once parts of larger rocks. The plant and animal materials come from plant and animal bodies.

No rock is so hard that it cannot in time be broken into pieces. The crumbling and wearing away of rock, which is called "weathering," goes on all the time and is done in many ways. Glaciers push great piles of rocks ahead of them as they move along and this pushing and grinding help crumble the rocks.

Water with chemicals in it will dissolve and wear away some kinds of rocks. Changes in temperature often help break rocks into small pieces. The heating and cooling of rocks may cause cracks to appear. Water gets into the cracks, freezes, and cracks the rocks even more. Even plant roots may cause rocks to break. Sometimes the seeds of trees fall into cracks in rocks, the seeds sprout, and as the roots of the plant grow, they help split the rock. Wind also helps crumble rocks by hurling sand against the rocks.

But this is only the beginning of soil-making. To make real soil, the sand or fine particles of rock must have "humus" added to it. Humus is an organic material that comes from plants and animal bodies. The bodies of almost all dead land plants and animals become a part of soil, through the work of bacteria.

Bacteria cause the plants and animals to decay and make the soil fertile. Earthworms and many kinds of insects help to make the soil rich. The richest layer of soil is at the top and is called "topsoil." This has much humus in it. The next layer, which is called "subsoil," contains mostly bits of rock. The layer beneath is bedrock, which is under the soil everywhere.

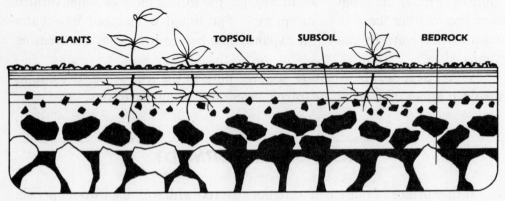

PLANTS   TOPSOIL   SUBSOIL   BEDROCK

WHAT IS SILVER?

The mining of silver has been carried on from ancient times. In Europe, kings depended on it as their source of wealth. In fact, when the Spanish silver mines began to run low, the King of Spain was delighted that the discovery of America led him to obtain the great silver mines of Mexico and Peru. The mines at Potosi in Peru produced $4,000,000 worth of silver every year for 250 years for the kings of Spain!

During the gold rush days in California, people cursed the "black earth" that stuck to their gold dust. It was only by accident that they discovered it was silver ore!

Silver is one of the most widely distributed of all metals. Sometimes it is found in solid pieces, and in Norway a piece of solid silver was once found that weighed three-quarters of a ton! But usually silver comes in ores from which it must be separated.

In this ore, silver is usually combined with sulphur as silver sulphide, or is a part of other sulphides, chiefly those of copper, lead, or arsenic. In the United States, it is found mostly in connection with lead. In fact, silver occurs in so many combinations that there are a great many different methods of separating it from the other elements.

Silver is too soft to be used in its pure state, so it is combined with other metals. Silver coins, for instance, contain 90 per cent silver and 10 per cent copper. The sterling silver of which jewelry and silverware are made contains 92.5 per cent silver and 7.5 per cent copper.

The name "sterling," by the way, has a curious origin. It comes from a North German family called Easterling. The Easterlings were such honest traders that King John of England gave them the job of making the English coins in 1215. They did it so well and truly that their name is still used as a sign of solid worth. All sterling silver is stamped with a hallmark, either the word "sterling" or a symbol, depending on the country.

Pure silver doesn't tarnish in pure air. When it turns black, that's a sign there is sulphur in the air, as from city smoke or oil wells. Next to gold, silver is the easiest metal to work with. One ounce of silver can be drawn into a wire more than 30 miles long! It is also the most perfect known conductor of electricity and heat.

WHY IS GOLD CONSIDERED PRECIOUS?

As far back as man has been known to exist, he has considered gold precious. It was probably the first metal known to man.

One reason primitive man was drawn to gold was that it can be found in the free state, which means gold can be found in small lumps (called "nuggets") uncombined with other metals or rocks. Since it has a bright yellow color and a shiny appearance, even the earliest man liked to possess it and make ornaments out of it.

The value of gold increased when people realized that it is the most easily worked of all metals. A nugget of gold is easily hammered thin and is flexible enough to bend without breaking. This means that early man could fashion gold into any shape he wished. At one time, for instance, it was used for hoops to bind the hair. Out of this came the idea of crowns and coronets made of gold.

The supply of gold that can be obtained easily from the earth is very limited. Soon people who couldn't find their own gold offered to exchange other things in return for some gold. That's how gold came to be a medium of exchange. While other commodities were perishable, gold was not, so it became a means of storing value for the future, and a measure of value, as well.

Centuries later, gold was made into coins as a convenient way of indicating the weight and fineness of the metal, and thus its value.

Later on, bankers would keep the gold itself in their vaults for safety's sake, and give a written pledge to deliver the gold on demand. From this practice, governments began to issue currency, or money, that was also simply a pledge to deliver a certain amount of gold on demand.

HOW HARD IS A DIAMOND?

If you had a piece of putty and wanted to make it hard, what would you do? You'd squeeze it and press it, and the more you squeezed and pressed, the harder it would become.

Diamonds were made in the same way by nature. A hundred million years ago, the earth was in its early cooling stages. At that time, there existed beneath the ground a mass of hot liquid rock. This was subjected to extreme heat and pressure. Carbon which was subjected to this pressure became what we called "diamonds."

Diamonds are the hardest natural substance known to man. But it is not very easy to measure "hardness" exactly. One way it is done is by using the scratch test, scratching it with another hard substance. In 1820, a man called Mohs made up a scale of hardness for minerals based on such a test. On his scale, this is the way the minerals ranked in hardness: 1. Talc. 2. Gypsum. 3. Calcite. 4. Fluorite. 5. Aphatite. 6. Feldspar. 7. Quartz. 8. Topaz. 9. Corundum. 10. Diamond.

But all this measured was how they compared to each other. For example, it has been found that even though corundum is 9 on the scale and diamond is 10, the difference between them in hardness is greater than the difference between 9 and 1 on the scale. So diamonds are the champions for hardness with no competition!

Since diamonds are so hard, how can they be shaped and cut? The only thing that will cut a diamond is another diamond! What diamond cutters use is a saw with an edge made of diamond dust.

In fact, diamond grinding and cutting wheels are used in industry in many ways, such as to grind lenses, to shape all kinds of tools made of copper, brass, and other metals, and to cut glass. Today, more than 80 per cent of all diamonds produced are used in industry!

WHAT IS RUBBER?

Rubber is as old as nature itself. Fossils have been found of rubber-producing plants that go back almost 3,000,000 years! Crude rubber balls have been found in the ruins of Incan and Mayan civilizations in Central and South America that are at least 900 years old.

In fact, when Columbus made his second voyage to the New World, he saw the natives of Haiti playing a game with a ball made from "the gum of a tree." And even before that, the natives of Southeastern Asia knew of rubber prepared from the "juice" of a tree and they used it to coat baskets and jars to make them waterproof!

Rubber has been found in more than 400 different vines, shrubs, and trees. But the amount of rubber found in each varies greatly and it doesn't pay to extract the rubber from such plants as dandelion, milkweed, and sagebrush.

Rubber is a sticky, elastic solid obtained from a milky liquid known as "latex," which is different from sap. The latex appears in the bark, roots, stem, branches, leaves, and fruit of plants and trees. But most of it is found in the inner bark of the branches and trunk of the rubber tree.

Latex consists of tiny particles of liquid, solid, or semi-fluid material which appear in a watery liquor. Only about 33 per cent of the latex is rubber; the rest is mostly water. The rubber particles in the latex are drawn together and a ball of rubber is formed.

Rubber grows best within 10 degrees of the Equator, and the area of about 700 miles on each side of the Equator is known as "the Rubber Belt." The reason for this is that the rubber tree needs a hot, moist climate and deep, rich soil. The best and most rubber comes from a tree called *Hevea brasiliensis*. As the name suggests this tree was first found in Brazil. Today almost 96 per cent of the world's supply of natural rubber comes from this tree, but now this tree is cultivated in many parts of the world within the Rubber Belt.

The first white men to manufacture rubber goods were probably the French, who made elastics for garters and suspenders some time before 1800.

WHAT IS CHALK?

Practically no one can grow up in the world today without coming into contact with chalk at some time in his life. In millions of classrooms around the world, children step up to blackboards to write things with chalk. And, of course, what could teacher do without chalk to help her?

Did you know that chalk was originally an animal? The waters of our oceans are covered with many forms of very tiny plants and animals. One of these is a one-celled animal called "Foraminifera." The shells of these creatures are made of lime.

When these animals die, their tiny shells sink to the floor of the ocean. In time, a thick layer of these shells is built up. Of course, this takes millions of years to accomplish. This layer gradually becomes cemented and compressed into a soft limestone which we call chalk.

As we know, various disturbances in the surface of the earth have often made dry land out of land that was once under water. One of the places where this happened is along the English Channel. The chalk layers at the bottom of the sea were pushed up. Later the soft parts were cut away by water, leaving huge cliffs of chalk. The two most famous ones are the chalk cliffs at Dover on the English side and at Dieppe on the French side of the Channel.

In other parts of the world, chalk deposits appear far inland in areas that were once under water. We have examples of these in our own country in Kansas, Arkansas, and Texas. But the finest natural chalk comes from England which produces more than 5,000,000 tons of it every year!

Chalk in one form or another has been used by man for hundreds of years. The blackboard chalk with which we are all familiar is mixed with some binding substance to prevent it from crumbling. The best blackboard chalk is about 95 per cent chalk. By adding pigments to it, chalk can be made in any color.

When chalk is pulverized, washed, and filtered, it is called "whiting." It can then be used in the making of many useful products such as putty, paints, medicines, paper, and toothpastes and powders!

WHAT IS CHLOROPHYLL?

If you had to pick the one chief thing that sets plants apart from animals, what would it be? The answer is that plants are green. Of course, there are some exceptions, but this is really the one basic law of plants—their greenness.

Now, this greenness of plants is one of the most important things in the entire world. Because the green coloring matter in plants—chlorophyll—enables them to take substances from the soil and the air and to manufacture living food. If plants couldn't do this, men and animals couldn't exist, for they would have no food! Even those creatures which live on meat depend on other creatures who live on plants. In fact, you can trace any food back to its original source and find it was made by a plant!

So you can see that chlorophyll, this miraculous green substance which enables plants to supply man and animals with food, is vital to our life, too! Chlorophyll is contained in the cells of leaves and often in the stem and flowers.

With the help of chlorophyll, the plant's living tissue is able to absorb the energy from sunlight and to use this energy to transform inorganic chemicals into organic or "life-giving" chemicals. This process is called "photosynthesis." The word comes from the Greek words which mean "light" and "put together."

There are some plants which have no green color, no chlorophyll. How do they live? Mushrooms, and a whole group of fungi, which have no chlorophyll, can't make their own food. So they have to get it in some way from something else. If they get their food from other plants or animals, they are called "parasites." If they get it from the decaying remains of plants and animals, they are called "saprophytes."

Chlorophyll can be extracted from plants and used in various ways by man. In such cases, it may help destroy certain bacteria.

WHAT IS A SEED?

One of the ways in which a plant produces another plant of its own kind is the seed. Just as birds lay eggs to reproduce their kind, the plant grows a seed that makes another plant.

The flower or blossom of a plant must be fertilized or the seed it produces will not grow. After the seed is fully grown, or mature, it must rest. The rest period varies among different kinds of seeds. Many of them will not grow until they have rested through the winter.

Seed growth requires moisture, oxygen, and warmth. Light helps some plants start seed growth. If seed growth doesn't start within a certain time, the seed will die. When seeds are stored by man for future use, they must be kept dry and within a certain temperature range.

Seeds vary greatly in size, shape, pattern, and color. The seeds of different plants are made in different ways. There is one kind of seed, for example, that has the tiny new plant in the center. Around this is stored food which will tide the young plant over until it has developed roots and leaves and can make its own food.

If a seed is fertile, has rested, and has received the proper amounts of moisture, oxygen, and warmth, it begins to grow. This is called "sprouting" or "germination." Growth often starts when moisture reaches the seed. As the seed absorbs water, it swells. As chemical changes take place, the cells of the seeds begin to show life again and the tiny young plant within the seed begins to grow. Most parts of the seed go into the growing plant. The seed cover drops off and the new plant grows larger until it matures and makes seeds of its own.

Seeds may be small or large. Begonia seeds are so small they look like dust. Coconuts are seeds which may weigh as much as 40 pounds! Some plants have only a few dozen seeds, while others, such as the maple, have thousands.

There are special ways seeds are made so that they will be spread. Burr-type seeds hitch a ride on the fur of animals. Seeds that stick in mud cling to animals' feet. Seeds contained in fruit are carried by man and animals. Some seeds have "wings" and are blown by the wind, other seeds float on water, and some are even "exploded" away from the parent plant!

HOW DO TREES GROW?

Like all living things, trees need nourishment in order to be able to grow. Where does the tree obtain this?

From the soil, the tree obtains water and minerals. From the air, it takes in carbon dioxide. And the green of the leaves of trees harnesses the energy of the sun's rays to make starches, sugars, and cellulose. So the tree carries on a chemical process of its own in order to be able to live and grow.

Between the wood of a tree and its bark, there is a thin band of living, dividing cells called "the cambium." As new cells are formed here, those that are formed on the wood side of the cambium mature as wood. The cells formed toward the outside mature as bark. In this way, as the tree grows older it increases in diameter.

The diameter of the woody part of the tree continues to grow greater and greater. But this doesn't always happen with the bark. Often the outer bark becomes broken, dies, and falls off.

Trees grow in height as well as in diameter. At the end of each branch or twig there is a group of living cells. During periods of active growth, these cells keep dividing, producing many more cells. These new cells enlarge and form new leaves as well as additional portions of the stem or twig. In this way, the twig grows longer.

After a time, these cells at the tip of the twig become less active and the twig grows longer more slowly. Then the new cells are firm and scale-like and they form a bud. You can easily notice these buds on trees during the winter.

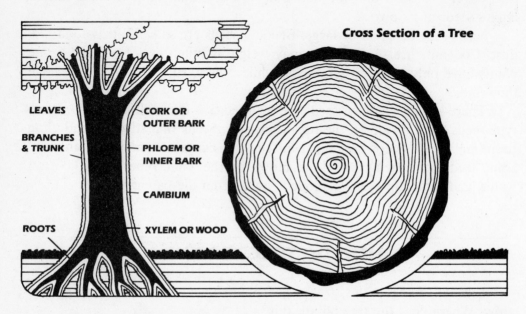

Cross Section of a Tree

LEAVES

BRANCHES & TRUNK

ROOTS

CORK OR OUTER BARK

PHLOEM OR INNER BARK

CAMBIUM

XYLEM OR WOOD

In the spring, the bud scales are spread apart or fall off and the twig starts growing longer again. So you see that by means of the cambium layer in the tree, and by means of the active cells at the tips of twigs, trees may grow both in thickness and in length, year after year.

A cross section of a tree shows alternating bands of light and dark wood. This difference in color is due to differences in size of the cells which make up the wood. The lighter bands have bigger cells which were formed in spring and early summer. The narrow dark bands are made up of smaller cells packed tightly together which were formed in late summer. Together, they show the amount of wood formed during a year, and by counting them, we can tell the age of a tree.

WHAT GIVES FLOWERS THEIR SCENT AND COLOR?

Curiously enough, we often look at a plant and admire its "flowers" when we are actually not looking at the flowers at all! If we think of a flower as something brightly colored which grows on a plant, we may be quite mistaken.

For instance, the "petals of the dogwood "blossoms" that bloom in the spring are not petals at all. Nor is the white sheath on a callas plant a flower. Poinsettia blossoms are another example of colored leaves rather than true flowers.

On the other hand, the bearded tufts at the tips of grasses are really flowers! An unripe ear of corn is actually a flower. According to the botanist, a flower is a group of parts whose function is to produce pollen or seeds or both. Only seed-bearing plants have flowers. And only those parts of a plant which are closely concerned with the formation and production of the seed can be considered as parts of the flower.

What gives flowers their scent? A flower has a fragrance when certain essential oils are found in the petals. These oils are produced by the plant as part of its growing process. These essential oils are very complex substances. Under certain conditions, this complex substance is broken down or decomposed and is formed into a volatile oil, which means it evaporates readily. When this happens, we can smell the fragrance it gives off.

The specific type of fragrance a flower gives off depends on the chemicals in that volatile oil, and various combinations produce different scents. By the way, these same oils are found not only in the flowers of plants but often in leaves, barks, roots, fruit, and seeds. For instance, oranges and lemons have them in the fruit, almonds have them in the seeds, cinnamon has them in the bark, and so on.

What gives flowers their color? "Anthocyanin" is the name for the pigments which give flowers the red, mauve, blue, purple, and violet colors. These pigments are dissolved in the sap of the cells of the flower. Other colors, such as yellow, orange, and green, are due to other pigments. These substances include chlorophyll, carotene, etc. There is no chemical link between them.

So we can attribute the colors in flowers to pigments called "anthocyanins" and to other pigments called "plastids." One group supplies a certain range of colors and the other group supplies the rest of the colors.

WHY DO LEAVES TURN DIFFERENT COLORS IN THE FALL?

When you look at a group of trees in the summertime, you see only one color: green. Of course, there are various shades of green, but it's as if it were all painted by one brush. Yet in the fall, these same leaves take on a whole variety of colors. Where do all these colors come from?

Well, to begin with, as most of us know, the green color of leaves is due to chlorophyll. Chlorophyll is the complete food factory that is found in each leaf. Two-thirds of the color of the leaves (their pigmentation) are due to this chlorophyll. There are other colors present in the leaf, too, but there is so much chlorophyll that we usually can't see them.

What are some of these other colors? A substance called "xanthophyll," which consists of carbon, hydrogen and oxygen, is yellow. It makes up about 23 per cent of the pigmentation of the leaf. Carotin, the substance which makes carrots the color they are, is also present in the leaf and makes up about 10 per cent of the pigment. Another pigment present is anthocyanin, which gives the sugar maple and the scarlet oak their bright red colors.

During the summer, we see none of these other pigments; we only see the green chlorophyll. When it becomes cold, the food that has been stored away in the leaf by the trees begins to flow out to the branches and trunks. Since no more food will be produced in the winter, the chlorophyll food factory closes down and the chlorophyll disintegrates. And as the chlorophyll disappears, the other pigments that have been present all the time become visible. The leaves take on all those beautiful colors which we enjoy seeing!

Before the leaves fall, a compact layer of cells is formed at the base of each leaf; then when the wind blows, the leaves are dislodged. On the twig there is a scar that marks the former position of each leaf.

Most evergreen trees do not shed all their leaves at the approach of winter, but lose them gradually through the year; thus they are always green.

HOW CAN YOU RECOGNIZE POISONOUS MUSHROOMS?

The best rule to follow about telling safe mushrooms from poisonous mushrooms is not to try! Despite what anyone may tell you, despite any "methods" you may know for telling them apart, you should never eat or even taste any mushroom that you find growing anywhere. The only safe mushrooms are those you buy in a food store!

There are a great many false ideas that people have about mushrooms. For example, some think that when poisonous mushrooms are cooked they will blacken a silver spoon if they are stirred with it. This "test" is wrong!

It is also untrue that certain mushrooms can harm you if you simply touch them. And there is no difference between a mushroom and a toadstool. They are simply two names for one thing!

Another false idea about mushrooms is that those with pink gills are safe to eat. This is based on the fact that the two best-known kinds which are safe to eat happen to have pink gills, and that the *Amanitas,* which are poisonous, have white gills. But the truth is that this difference between the two kinds can't always be detected. Besides, many safe mushrooms have gills that are not pink at all.

WHAT IS AN ACID?

Now and then, we read a newspaper story about someone being terribly burned by an acid. In fact, most of us think of acids as dangerous liquids which can burn the skin and eat holes in clothing.

This is only true of a very small number of acids. There are many acids in foods, and they are necessary for good health. Other acids are used to make drugs, paints, cosmetics, and industrial products.

There are many kinds of acids but they all may be divided into two classes, inorganic acids and organic acids. Here is a brief description of some of the more important acids in each group.

Sulphuric acid is an important industrial acid. It can cause severe damage to the eyes and serious burns on the skin. Hydrochloric acid is another very strong acid. It can be made from sulphuric acid and common table salt. It is used to make other chemicals and is very good for cleaning metals. The human body makes a small amount of weak hydrochloric acid, which helps in digestion.

Nitric acid is another powerful acid which can harm the skin and eyes. Boric acid, on the other hand, is a very weak acid. It occurs naturally in Italy. It is used to make ceramics, cements, pigments, and cosmetics. It is sometimes used as a germ-killer, but is not very good for this purpose. Carbonic acid comes from carbon dioxide gas, and there is some of it in the soda pop we drink. Arsenic acid is used to make insect-killing products.

Organic acids are not as strong as inorganic acids. Acetic acid is found in vinegar, and can be made by fermenting apple cider. When sugar ferments in milk, lactic acid is formed. It turns the milk sour, but it is also used in making cheese.

Amino acids are needed to keep the body in good health, and they come from protein foods. Oranges, lemons, and grapefruit contain ascorbic acid, which is the chemical name for Vitamin C. Liver, poultry, and beef contain nicotinic acid, which helps prevent skin diseases.

So you see that the story of acids is a long and complicated one. Some are dangerous to human beings, but useful in industry. Some are necessary for human life and are supplied by various foods. Some are made by the body itself to keep it functioning.

WHAT IS ASBESTOS?

Many people think asbestos is a modern invention, but it has actually been known and used for thousands of years! In ancient temples, it was used for torch wicks and to protect fires lit on the altars. The Romans used asbestos 2,000 years ago for winding sheets to preserve the ashes of the dead when bodies were cremated. There is even a legend that Charlemagne had an asbestos tablecloth. He laundered it by putting it in the fire to burn off stains.

Asbestos is a Greek word that means "inextinguishable" or "unquenchable." Today we apply it to a group of fibrous minerals which have the property of resisting fire. The minerals that make up asbestos differ widely in composition, and each has a different strength, flexibility, and usefulness. From the chemical point of view, asbestos usually consists of silicates of lime and magnesia and sometimes contains iron.

Because it is made up of fibers, asbestos is similar to cotton and wool, but asbestos has the added advantage of being heat- and fire-resistant. This makes it very valuable for many uses in industry, and science has not yet been able to find a substitute for it.

No other mineral we know can be spun into yarn or thread, woven into cloth, or made into sheets. Workers in plants who are exposed to risks of fire sometimes wear complete outfits made of asbestos, including helmets, gloves, suits, and boots. Asbestos can withstand temperatures of 2,000 to 3,000 degrees Fahrenheit, and there are some kinds of asbestos that can even resist temperatures as high as 5,000 degrees!

Asbestos is found in veins in certain types of rocks, and sometimes it's necessary to mine and treat as much as 50 tons of rock to produce one ton of asbestos fiber!

WHAT CAUSES THE TOWER OF PISA TO LEAN?

When something captures the imagination of the world, it is remembered by people far more than things that may be more important. Everybody knows that in the city of Pisa in Italy, there is a tower that "leans." Very few people know that this town has a great and glorious history.

Of course, the tower itself is quite a marvel, too. It is built entirely of white marble. The walls are 13 feet thick at its base. It has eight storeys and is 179 feet high, which in our country would be about the height of a 15-storey building.

There is a stairway built into the walls consisting of 300 steps, which leads to the top. And by the way, those people who climb these stairs to the top get a magnificent view of the city and of the sea, which is six miles away.

At the top, the tower is 16½ feet out of the perpendicular. In other words, it "leans" over by 16½ feet. If you were to stand at the top and drop a stone to the ground, it would hit 16½ feet away from the wall at the bottom of the tower!

What makes it lean? Nobody really knows the answer. Of course, it wasn't supposed to lean when it was built; it was supposed to stand straight. It was intended as a bell-tower for the cathedral which is nearby and was begun in 1174 and finished in 1350.

The foundations of the tower were laid in sand, and this may explain why it leans. But it didn't suddenly begin to lean—this began to happen when only three of its storeys, or "galleries," had been built. So the plans were changed slightly and construction went right on! In the last hundred years, the tower has leaned another foot. According to some engineers, it should be called "the falling tower," because they believe that it will eventually topple over.

Did you know that Galileo, who was born in Pisa, is said to have performed some of his experiments concerning the speed of falling bodies at this tower?

DO THE NORTHERN LIGHTS APPEAR IN THE SOUTH?

The northern lights, or the aurora borealis, is one of nature's most dazzling spectacles.

When it appears, there is often a crackling sound coming from the sky. A huge, luminous arc lights up the night, and this arc is constantly in motion. Sometimes, the brilliant rays of light spread upward in the shape of a fan. At other times, they flash here and there like giant searchlights, or move up and down so suddenly that they have been called "the merry dancers."

Farther north, the aurora frequently looks like vast, fiery draperies which hang from the sky and sway to and fro while flames of red, orange, green, and blue play up and down the moving folds.

According to scientific measurements, this discharge of light takes place from 50 to 100 miles above the earth. But it doesn't reach its greatest brilliance at the North Pole. It is seen at its best around the Hudson Bay region in Canada, in northern Scotland, and in southern Norway and Sweden. It may sometimes be seen even in the United States as it flashes across the northern sky.

We call this "the northern lights," or "aurora borealis." But such lights occur in the Southern Hemisphere, too! They are known as "the aurora australis." In fact, sometimes both lights are called "aurora polaris."

Science is still not certain regarding exactly what these lights are and what causes them. But it is believed that the rays are due to discharges of electricity in the rare upper atmosphere.

The displays seem to center about the earth's magnetic poles, and electrical and magnetic disturbances often occur when the lights are especially brilliant. They also seem to be related to sunspots in some unknown way.

If nearly all the air is pumped out of a glass tube, and a current of electricity is then passed through the rarefied gases, there will be a display of lights inside the tube. The aurora displays seen high above the earth may be caused by the same phenomenon, electrical discharges from the sun passing through rarefied gases.

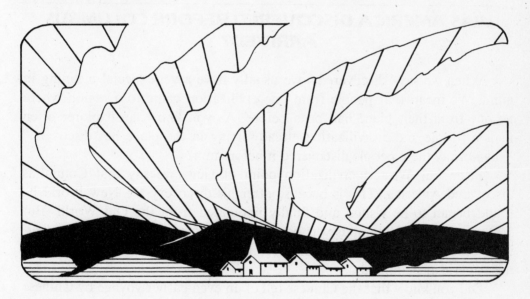

CHAPTER 2
HOW THINGS BEGAN

WAS AMERICA DISCOVERED BEFORE COLUMBUS ARRIVED?

When we say "discovered," we usually have a very special meaning in mind. We mean that people from one civilization came to a region where no one from their place had been before. As you know, an explorer often finds a people and a civilization already living in the place he "discovers." Why not say these people discovered it before him?

From our Western-civilization point of view, we say that Columbus discovered America. This is because after his discovery the New World he found began to be visited and finally populated from the Old World. But 500 years before Columbus was born, the Norsemen did a bit of "discovering," too. They sailed west to discover Iceland, then Greenland, and later the American mainland.

Did you know that the Chinese tell of an even earlier voyage by Chinese sailors to discover what has become California? And people of the South Sea Islands still sing of the great men of their distant past who sailed to South America long before the white man reached either South America or the South Sea Islands.

For all we know, there may have been many ages of exploration thousands of years ago. There were certainly ages of exploration before the time of Columbus. Perhaps we might say that neither Columbus, nor the Norsemen before him, "discovered" America. Weren't the Indians already living here for many centuries before the white man arrived?

And who can say that they didn't set out on a voyage of discovery? It is believed that they came from Asia, though we don't know when or how they made the trip. Probably they reached America over a period of centuries and by different routes. They also probably sent their scouts ahead to seek out routes by land or sea. These scouts were their explorers, and perhaps it was really they who discovered America!

WHAT IS EVOLUTION?

In trying to explain the existence of the complicated body structures we see in living things around us, a theory of evolution has been developed. While most scientists accept this theory, many people do not. They feel it goes against what is written in the Bible.

This theory is that all the plants and animals in the world today have developed in a natural way from earlier forms that were simpler. These earlier forms developed from still simpler ancestors, and so on back through millions of years to the very beginning when life was in its simplest form, merely a tiny mass of jellylike protoplasm.

According to this theory, man, too, developed from some simpler form, just as the modern one-hoofed horse is the descendant of a small five-toed ancestor.

In trying to prove that evolution did take place, scientists depend on three chief "signs." One of these is the study of fossil remains of animals and plants of past ages. Some of these fossils seem to trace the steps of evolution at work. Fossil remains of primitive men have been found that go back to a time 1,000,000 years ago. Fossils of certain crablike animals go back nearly 500,000,000 years. These fossils show that fish developed in the waters of the earth before amphibians, amphibians before reptiles, reptiles before birds, and so on. Scientists believe this proves life has progressed from one form to another.

Another "sign" of evolution comes from the study of embryology, the growth of a new living thing from an egg. In studying the development of the chick from the hen's egg, there is a time when this embryo is like a fish, later it's like an amphibian, then it passes through the reptile stage, and finally develops into its bird form. The unborn young of all animals go through the same kind of process, repeating their history of development.

The third "sign" is the bodies of living animals. For example, the bone and muscle structure in the paddles of a turtle, the wings of a bird, the flippers of a whale, the front legs of a horse, and the arms of a man are similar in structure. And man has many organs in his body which seem of no use. They are thought to be relics handed down from his earlier ancestors. These are some of the "signs" that led to a theory of evolution.

HOW LONG HAVE PEOPLE BEEN USING LAST NAMES?

"Hey, Shorty!" "Hi, Skinny." "There's Fatso." "Here comes Blondie." Sound familiar to you? It's a perfectly natural way to call people—give them a name that describes them in some way.

And you know, that's exactly the way first names were given originally! A girl born during a famine might be called Una (Celtic for "famine"), a golden haired blonde might be called Blanche (French for "white"). A boy might be called David because it means "beloved."

A first name was all anybody had for thousands of years. Then, about the time the Normans conquered England in 1066, last names, or surnames, were added to identify people better. The first name wasn't enough to set one person apart from another. For example, there might be two Davids in town, and one of them was quite lazy. So people began to call this one "David, who is also lazy," or "David do little." And this became David Doolittle.

The last names were originally called "ekenames." The word "eke" meant "also." And by the way, we get our word "nickname" from this word!

Once people got into the habit of giving a person two names, they thought of many ways of creating this second name. For example, one way was to mention the father's name. If John had a father called William, he might be called John Williamson, or John Williams, or John Wilson (Will's son), or John Wills.

Another good way to identify people with second names was to mention the place where they lived or came from. A person who lived near the woods might be called Wood, or if he lived near the village green he might be called John Green.

And then, of course, the work that a person did was a good way to identify him. So we have last names like Smith, Taylor, and Wright. ("Wright" means someone who does mechanical work.)

The nearest thing to last names in ancient times existed among the Romans. A second name was sometimes added to indicate the family or clan to which a child belonged. Later, they even added a third name, which was a kind of descriptive nickname.

HOW DID THE CUSTOM OF KISSING START?

We know the kiss as a form of expressing affection. But long before it became this, it was the custom in many parts of the world to use the kiss as an expression of homage.

In many African tribes the natives kiss the ground over which a chief has walked. Kissing the hand and foot has been a mark of respect and homage from the earliest times. The early Romans kissed the mouth or eyes as a form of dignified greeting. One Roman emperor allowed his important nobles to kiss his lips, but the less important ones had to his kiss his hands, and the least important ones were only allowed to kiss his feet!

It is quite probable that the kiss as a form of affection can be traced back to primitive times when a mother would fondle her child, just as a mother does today. It only remained for society to accept this as a custom for expressing affection between adults.

We have evidence that this was already the case by the time of the sixth century, but we can only assume it was practiced long before that. The first country where the kiss became accepted in courtship and love was in France. When dancing became popular, almost every dance figure ended with a kiss.

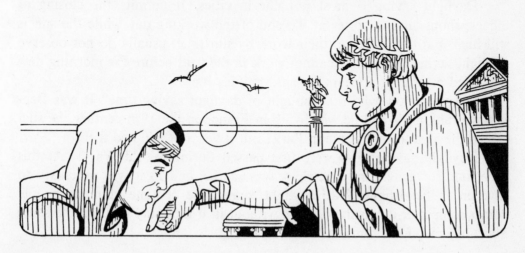

From France the kiss spread rapidly all over Europe. Russia, which loved to copy the customs of France, adopted the kiss and it spread there through all the upper classes. A kiss from the Tsar became one of the highest form of recognition from the Crown.

In time, the kiss became a part of courtship. As marriage customs developed, the kiss became a part of the wedding ceremony. Today, of course, we regard the kiss an an expression of love and tenderness. But there are still many places in the world where the kiss is part of formal ceremonies and is intended to convey respect and homage.

WHY DO WE HAVE DAYLIGHT SAVING TIME?

Let's say a person gets up at 7:00 in the morning and goes to bed at 11:00 at night. He comes home from work about 6:30, and by the time he's finished with dinner it's after 8:00. He steps outside in the summer to relax—but it's already getting dark! Not much time to enjoy the summer day.

Now suppose you set the clock ahead one hour. This person still does everything at the same hour—but this time, when he steps out at 8:00 o'clock there's still plenty of light to enjoy. An hour of daylight has been "saved" for him!

Daylight saving time doesn't, of course, add any hours to a day. That's impossible. All it does is increase the number of useful hours of daylight during the seasons when the sun rises early.

Daylight saving is most popular in cities. It permits the closing of offices, shops, and factories at the end of the working day while the sun is still high. Farmers, who do their work by sun time, usually do not observe daylight saving time. They cannot work in the field before the morning dew has dried or after it appears in the evening.

Did you know who first thought of daylight saving time? It was Benjamin Franklin! When he was living in France in the 18th century, he suggested the idea to the people in Paris. But it was not adopted then.

Daylight saving laws were first passed during World War I. At this time, fuel for generating electricity was scarce, and so it was necessary to save on artificial light. With daylight saving, the bedtime of many people comes soon after it gets dark, while without it, if they stay up until the same hour they may have to use artificial light.

The first country to adopt daylight saving time was Germany in 1915. Then England used it in 1916, and the United States adopted it in 1918.

During World War II, the United States put it in force again on a national basis, and this ended at the close of the war.

HOW DID THE CALENDAR BEGIN?

When men first began to plant seeds and harvest crops, they noticed that the time for planting came at a regular time each year. Then they tried to count how many days came between one planting time and the next. This was man's first attempt to find out how long a year was!

The ancient Egyptians were the first to measure a year with any exactness. They knew that the best time to plant was right after the Nile River overflowed each year. Their priests noticed that between each overflowing the moon rose 12 times. So they counted 12 *moonths* or months, and figured out when the Nile would rise again.

But it still wasn't exact enough. At last the Egyptian priests noticed that each year, about the time of the flood, a certain bright star would rise just before the sun rose. They counted the days that passed before this happened again and found that it added up to 365 days. This was 6000 years ago, and before that no one had ever known that there were 365 days in a year! The Egyptians divided this year into 12 months of 30 days each, with 5 extra days at the end of the year. Thus they invented the first calendar.

Eventually, the calendar was based not on the moon (lunar calendar) but on the number of days ($365\frac{1}{4}$) it takes the earth to go around the sun (solar calendar). The extra quarter of day began to cause more and more confusion. Finally, Julius Caesar decided to straighten it all out. He ordered that the year 46 B.C. should have 445 days to "catch up," and that every year from then on was to have 365 days, except every fourth year. This fourth year would have a leap year of 366 days to use up the fraction left over in each ordinary year.

But as time went on it was discovered that Easter and other holy days were not coming where they belonged in the seasons. Too many "extra" days had piled up. In the year 1582, Pope Gregory XIII decided to do something about it. He ordered that ten days should be dropped from the year 1582. And to keep the calendar accurate for all future time, he ordered that leap year should be skipped in the last year of every century unless that year could be divided by 400. Thus 1700, 1800, and 1900 were not leap years, but the year 2000 will be a leap year!

This system is called the Gregorian calendar and is now used all over the world for everyday purposes, though various religions still use their own calendar for religious purposes!

HOW DID THE DAYS OF THE WEEK GET THEIR NAMES?

There was a time in the early history of man when the days had no names! The reason was quite simple. Men had not invented the week.

In those days, the only division of times was the month, and there were too many days in the month for each of them to have a separate name. But when men began to build cities, they wanted to have a special day on which to trade, a market day. Sometimes these market days were fixed at every tenth day, sometimes every seventh or every fifth day. The Babylonians decided that it should be every seventh day. On this day they didn't work, but met for trade and religious festivals.

The Jews followed their example, but kept every seventh day for religious purposes. In this way the week came into existence. It was the space between market days. The Jews gave each of the seven days a name, but it was really a number after the Sabbath day (which was Saturday). For example, Wednesday was called the fourth day (four days after Saturday).

When the Egyptians adopted the seven-day week, they named the days after five planets, the sun, and the moon. The Romans used the Egyptian names for their days of the week: the day of the sun, of the moon, of the planet Mars, of Mercury, of Jupiter, of Venus, and of Saturn.

We get our names for the days not from the Romans but from the Anglo-Saxons, who called most of the days after their own gods, which were roughly the same as the gods of the Romans. The day of the sun became *Sunnandaeg*, or Sunday. The day of the moon was called *Monandaeg*, or Monday. The day of Mars became the day of Tiw, who was their god of war. This became *Tiwesdaeg*, or Tuesday. Instead of Mercury's name, that of the god Woden was given to Wednesday. The Roman day of Jupiter, the thunderer, became the day of the thunder god Thor, and this became Thursday. The next day was named for Frigg, the wife of their god Odin, and so we have Friday. The day of Saturn became *Saeternsdaeg*, a translation from the Roman, and then Saturday.

A day, by the way, used to be counted as the space between sunrise and sunset. The Romans counted it as from midnight to midnight, and most modern nations use this method.

WHY ARE EGGS AND RABBITS ASSOCIATED WITH EASTER?

Easter is the most joyous of Christian holidays. It is celebrated in commemoration of the Resurrection of Jesus Christ.

The exact day on which Easter falls may vary from year to year, but it always comes, of course, in the spring of the year. Thus, as Christianity spread, the celebration of Easter included many customs that were linked with the celebration of spring's arrival. This explains why many Easter customs go back to traditions that existed before Christianity itself.

Both Easter and the coming of spring are symbols of new life. The ancient Egyptians and Persians celebrated their spring festivals by coloring and eating eggs. This is because they considered the egg a symbol of fertility and new life. The Christians adopted the egg as symbolic of new life, the symbol of the Resurrection.

There is another reason why we observe the practice of eating eggs on Easter Sunday and of giving them as gifts to friends or children. In the early days of the Church, eggs were forbidden food during Lent. With the ending of Lent, people were so glad to see and eat eggs again that they made it a tradition to eat them on Easter Sunday.

The Easter hare also was part of the spring celebrations long before Christianity. In the legends of ancient Egypt, the hare is associated with the moon. The hare is linked with the night because it comes out only then to feed. By being associated with the moon, the hare became a symbol of a new period of life. Thus the hare stood for the renewal of life and for fertility. The early Christians therefore took it over and linked it with Easter, the holiday that symbolizes new life!

By the way, the tradition of wearing new clothes on Easter Sunday is also symbolic of casting off the old and the beginning of the new!

HOW DID HALLOWEEN ORIGINATE?

The name Halloween means "hallowed, or holy, evening." Yet, for some reason this holiday has become one of the most popular and best liked holidays of the entire year and is celebrated with great enthusiasm in many countries.

Halloween, which takes place on October 31st, is really a festival to celebrate autumn, just as May Day is a festival to celebrate spring. The ancient Druids (the Druids were the religious priests in ancient Gaul, Britain, and Ireland) had a great festival to celebrate autumn which began at midnight on October 31st and lasted through the next day, November 1st.

They believed that on this night their great god of death, called Saman, called together all the wicked souls who had died during the year and whose punishment had been to take up life in the bodies of animals. Of course, the very idea of such a gathering was enough to frighten the simple-minded people of that time. So they lit huge bonfires and kept a sharp watch for these evil spirits. This is actually where the idea that witches and ghosts are about on Halloween began. And there are still people in certain isolated parts of Europe who believe this to be true!

The Romans also had a holiday about the 1st of November which was in honour of their goddess Pomona. Nuts and apples were roasted before great bonfires. Our own Halloween seems to be a combination of the Roman and Druid festivals.

Originally, the Halloween festival was quite simple and was celebrated mostly in church. But all over Europe, people looked upon this occasion as an opportunity to have fun and excitement, to tell spooky tales, and to scare each other. So instead of being devoted to the celebration of autumn, it became a holiday devoted to the supernatural, to witches, and to ghosts.

Here are some of the curious customs which sprang up in connection with Halloween: Young girls who "ducked" for apples on this night could see their future husbands if they slept with the apple under their pillow. Stealing gates, furniture, signs, and so on, is done to make people think they were stolen by the evil spirits. And, of course, no one goes near a cemetery on Halloween because spirits rise up on that night! Today we use these superstitions as a way of having fun on Halloween.

WHO FIRST THOUGHT OF THE ALPHABET?

The letters of an alphabet are really sound signs. Those of the English alphabet are based on the Roman alphabet, which is about 2,500 years old. The capital letters are almost exactly like those used in Roman inscriptions of the third century B.C.

Before alphabets were invented men used pictures to record events or communicate ideas. A picture of several antelopes might mean "Here are good hunting grounds," so this was really a form of writing. Such "picture writing" was highly developed by the ancient Babylonians, Egyptians, and Chinese.

In time, picture writing underwent a change. The picture, instead of just standing for the object that was drawn, came to represent an idea connected with the object drawn. For example, the picture of a foot might indicate the verb "to walk." This stage of writing is called "ideographic," or "idea writing."

The trouble with this kind of writing was that the messages might be interpreted by different people in different ways. So little by little this method was changed. The symbols came to represent combinations of sounds. For example, if the word for "arm" were "id," the picture of an arm would stand for the sound of "id." So the picture of an arm was used every time they wanted to convey the sound "id." This stage of writing might be called "syllabic writing."

The Babylonians and Chinese and the Egyptians never passed beyond this stage of writing. The Egyptians did make up a kind of alphabet by including among their pictures 24 signs which stood for separate letters or words of one consonant each. But they didn't realize the value of their invention.

About 3,500 years ago, people living near the eastern shore of the Mediterranean made the great step leading to our alphabet. They realized that the same sign could be used for the same sound in all cases, so they used a limited number of signs in this manner and these signs made up an alphabet.

A development of their alphabet was used by the Hebrews and later the Phoenicians. The Phoenicians carried their alphabet to the Greeks. The Romans adopted the Greek alphabet with certain changes and additions and handed it down to the people of Western Europe in the Latin alphabet. From this came the alphabet we use today.

WHY DON'T WE ALL SPEAK THE SAME LANGUAGE?

At one time, at the beginning of history, what there was of mankind then probably spoke one language. As time went on, this parent language, or perhaps there were several parent languages, spread and changed.

At first, the parent languages were spoken by small numbers of persons or by scattered small groups. Gradually, some groups increased in numbers and there wasn't enough food for all of them. So some people would form a band to move to a new location.

When these people arrived at a new location and settled down, they would speak almost the same as the people from whom they had parted. Gradually, though, new pronunciations would creep in. The people would begin to say things a little differently and there would be changes in the sounds of words.

Some words that were needed in the old home were no longer needed in the new place and would be dropped. New experiences would require new words to describe them. Ways of making sentences would change. And suppose the people had settled in a place where others were already living? The two languages would blend, and thus both of the old languages would change.

At first, when the speech of the new people had changed only slightly from the original language, it would be called "a dialect." After a longer time, when there were many changes in words, sounds, and grammar, it would be considered a new language.

In just these ways, Spanish, French, and Portuguese developed from Latin; and English, Norwegian, Swedish, Danish, and Dutch grew from an early form of the German language.

The ancestor language, together with all the languages which developed from it, is called "a family" of languages.

HOW DID THE ENGLISH LANGUAGE BEGIN?

Practically all languages spoken on earth today can be traced by scholars back to some common source, that is, an ancestor language which has many descendants. The ancestor language—together with all the languages which have developed from it—is called a "family" of languages.

English is considered a member of the Indo-European family of languages. Other languages belonging to the same family are French, Italian, German, Norwegian, and Greek.

In this Indo-European family of languages there are various branches and English is a member of the "West Teutonic" branch. Actually, English dates from about the middle of the fifth century, when invaders from across the North Sea conquered the native Celts and settled on the island now known as England.

For the sake of convenience, the history of the English language is divided into three great periods: the old English (or Anglo-Saxon), from about 400 to 1100; Middle English, from 1100 to 1500; and Modern English, from 1500 to the present day.

So the original language spoken in English was Celtic. But the Anglo-Saxons (the Angles, the Jutes, and the Saxons) conquered the island so thoroughly that very few Celtic words were kept in the new language.

The Anglo-Saxons themselves spoke several dialects. Later on, the Norsemen invaded England and they introduced a Scandinavian element into the language. This influence, which was a Germanic language, became a part of the language.

In 1066, William the Conqueror brought over still another influence to the language. He made Norman French the language of his Court. At first, this "Norman" language was spoken only by the upper classes. But gradually its influence spread and a language quite different from the Anglo-Saxon developed. This language became the chief source of modern English.

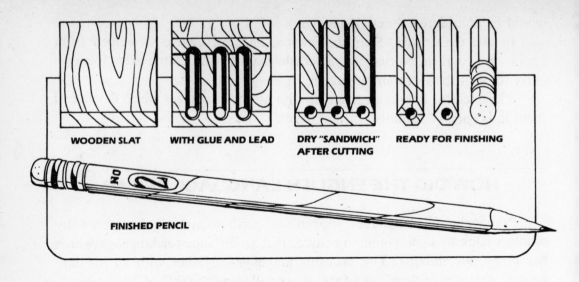

WOODEN SLAT   WITH GLUE AND LEAD   DRY "SANDWICH"   READY FOR FINISHING
AFTER CUTTING

FINISHED PENCIL

WHO INVENTED THE PENCIL?

There is a Latin word, *penicillus,* which means "little tail." This word was used to indicate a fine brush, and the word "pencil" originally meant a small, fine pointed brush.

Today, of course, a pencil means something altogether different. Pencils as we know them are less than 200 years old. About 500 years ago, graphite was discovered in a mine in Cumberland, England, and it is believed that some sort of crude pencils may have been made then.

In Nuremberg, Germany, the famous Faber family established its business in 1760 and used pulverized graphite to make a kind of pencil, but they were not very successful. Finally in 1795, a man called N. J. Conte produced pencils made of graphite which had been ground with certain clays, pressed into sticks, and fired in a kiln. This method is the basis for the manufacture of all modern pencils.

As you might have guessed by now, a "lead" pencil doesn't contain lead but a mineral substance called graphite. Graphite, like lead, leaves a mark when drawn across paper. Because of this it is called "black lead," and that's where we get the name "lead pencil."

In manufacturing pencils, dried ground graphite is mixed with clay and water. The more clay, the harder the pencil will be; the more graphite, the softer the pencil. After the mixture reaches a doughy consistency, it passes through a forming press and comes out as a thin, sleek rope. This is straightened out, cut into lengths, dried, and put into huge ovens to bake.

Meanwhile, the pencil case has been prepared. The wood, either red cedar or pine, is shaped in halves and grooved to hold the lead. After the finished leads are inserted in the grooves, the halves of the pencil are glued together. A saw cuts the slats into individual pencils, and a shaping machine gives the surface a smooth finish.

Today, more than 350 different kinds of pencils are made, each for a special use. You can buy black lead pencils in 19 degrees of hardness and intensity, or get them in 72 different colors! There are pencils that write on glass, cloth, cellophane, plastics, and movie film. There are even pencils, used by engineers and in outdoor construction work, that leave a mark that won't fade after years of exposure to any weather!

WHO DISCOVERED HOW TO MAKE PAPER?

Take a piece of paper and tear it in both directions. You will notice two things. It tore more easily in one direction than in the other, and hairlike fibers stick out from the edges of the tear.

The first shows that the paper was made by machine; otherwise it would tear the same way in all directions. The second shows that paper is a mat of tiny fibers, felted together. These fibers are the small particles of cellulose that help form the framework of plants.

Man had created a writing material before he invented paper. The ancient Egyptians, about 4000 years ago, took the stems of the papyrus plant and peeled them apart and flattened them. Then they laid them crosswise and pressed them down to stick them together. When dry, this made a sheet of papyrus and could be written on.

But it wasn't paper. This was invented in China about the year 105, by a man called Ts'ai Lun. He found a way to make paper from the stringy inner bark of the mulberry tree.

The Chinese pounded the bark in water to separate the fibers, then poured the soup mixture onto a tray with a bottom of thin bamboo strips. The water drained away and the soft mat was laid on a smooth surface to dry. Bamboo and old rags were also used. Later on, somebody thought how to improve the paper by brushing starch on it.

Chinese traders traveled far to the west and came to the city of Samarkand in Russia. There they met Arabs who learned their secret and took it to Spain. From there the art of papermaking spread over Europe and to England.

In time, all kinds of improved methods and machines for making paper were discovered. One of the most important, for example, was a machine developed in France in 1798 that could make a continuous sheet or web of paper.

WHEN WERE BOOKS FIRST MADE?

Books as we know them didn't appear until the Middle Ages. The nearest thing to them were rolls of papyrus. Sheets of papyrus were glued together to form long rolls. The Romans called them *volumen,* from which we get our word "volume."

About the middle of the fifth century, parchment and vellum had replaced papyrus. Parchment is made from the skins of sheep and goats and vellum is made from calfskin. Sheets of this material, with writing on one side, were cut to uniform size and bound together at one side with leather tongs. So they were "books" in a way.

But it was in the Middle Ages that books were first made that resemble our printed books of today. Four pieces of vellum were folded in such a way so that each piece formed two leaves. These pieces were then placed inside one another so that there was a group of eight leaves, which is called "a section."

These sections were sent to a scribe to write the book. He took them apart and wrote a single page at a time. Vellum was thick enough so there could be writing on both sides.

The next step was to send the finished sections that made up the book to the binder. He sewed the sections through the back fold with cords. Wooden covers were made and the ends were laced through holes in the boards to bind together the sections and the covers. Then a large piece of leather was glued over the back of the sections and the wooden sides. Other steps were taken to decorate and preserve these books, but these were the first books that resemble those we have today.

Most of the medieval books were Bibles, sermons, and other religious books. Next came books of law, medicine, natural history, and later came a few chronicles and romances. Most books of the Middle Ages are in Latin.

WHO INVENTED CARTOONS?

You know that between the way something started years ago, and the way it is today, there may be quite a difference! There is no better example of this than the cartoon.

The word "cartoon" was originally used by painters during the period of the Italian Renaissance. And in fact, it is still used today by artists. What they are referring to, however, is the first sketch in actual size of any work of art which covers a large area, such as a mural, a tapestry, or a stained-glass window.

When newspapers and magazines began to use drawings to illustrate news and editorial opinion and to provide amusement, these drawings also came to be called "cartoons"!

In the days before newspapers, famous caricaturists like Hogarth, Goya, Daumier, and Rowlandson made series of drawings on a single theme. These drawings often pictured the adventures of one character. They were the ancestors of present-day cartoons and comic strips.

In the 19th and early 20th century there were a number of magazines which specialized in cartoons—*Charivari* in Paris, *Punch* in London, and *Life* and *Judge* in the United States. When most newspapers and magazines in the United States began to include cartoons as regular features, the humorous magazines lost their appeal and many of them stopped appearing.

The first comic strips appeared in the early 1900's. Richard Outcault, the artist who created *Buster Brown,* published this comic strip in 1902. It was so popular that children all over the country wanted to dress in "Buster Brown" clothes.

Another of the early comic strips was *Bringing Up Father*. This came out in 1912. It has since been translated into 27 different languages, and published in 71 countries!

HOW DID OUR SYSTEM OF COUNTING BEGIN?

It seems very natural to you that if you have two pennies and you add two pennies to them, you have four pennies. But did you know it may have taken man millions of years to be able to think this way? In fact, one of the most difficult things to teach children is the concept of numbers.

In ancient times, when a man wanted to tell how many animals he owned, he had no system of numbers to use. What he did was put a stone or pebble into a bag for each animal. The more animals, the more stones he had. Which may explain why our word "calculate" comes from the Latin word *calculus* which means "stone"!

Later on, man used tally marks to count. He would just scratch a line or tally mark for each object he wanted to count, but he had no word to tell the number.

The next step in the development of the number system was probably the use of fingers. And again we have a word that goes back to this. The word "digit" comes from the Latin word *digitus,* which means "finger"! And since we have 10 fingers, this led to the general use of "10" in systems of numbers.

But in ancient times there was no single number system used all over the world. Some number systems were based on 12, others were based on 60, others on 20, and still others on 2, 5, and 8. The system invented by the Romans about 2,000 years ago was widely used by the people of Europe until about the 16th century. In fact, we still use it on clocks and to show chapters in books. But it was a very complicated system.

The number system we use today was invented by the Hindus in India thousands of years ago and was brought to Europe about the year 900 by Arab traders. In this system all numbers are written with the nine digits 1, 2, 3, 4, 5, 6, 7, 8, 9 to show how many, and the zero. It is a decimal system, that is, it is built on the base 10.

WHAT MAKES MONEY VALUABLE?

The idea of having such a thing as money is one of the most fascinating ever developed by man. But many people don't know where this idea came from, or why money is valuable.

Thousands of years ago, money was not used. Instead, man had the "barter" system. This meant that if a man wanted something he didn't happen to make or raise himself, he had to find someone who had this article. Then he had to offer him something in exchange. And if the man didn't like what he offered in exchange, he couldn't get his article!

In time, certain things came to be used as money because practically everyone would take these things in exchange. For example, cows, tobacco,

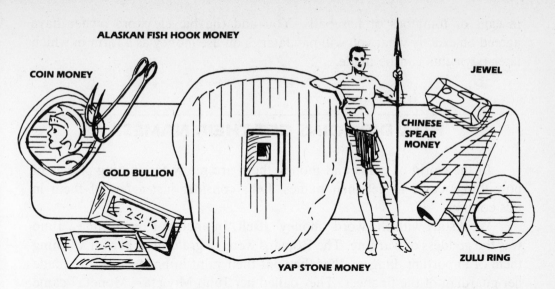

COIN MONEY

ALASKAN FISH HOOK MONEY

GOLD BULLION

24.K

24.K

YAP STONE MONEY

JEWEL

CHINESE SPEAR MONEY

ZULU RING

grains, skins, salt, and beads were all used as money among people who were always ready to accept them.

Eventually, all these varieties of money were replaced by pieces of metal, especially gold and silver. Later on, coins were made of a certain purity and weight, and these represented certain amounts of various objects. So many coins represented a cow, or 50 pounds of tobacco, and so on.

Today, of course, we have bills and coins issued by the Government, and everybody accepts and uses this money. What makes the money valuable, what use does it have for us? There are four chief things that money does for you.

First, it makes possible exchange and trade. Suppose you want a bicycle. You're willing to work for it by mowing lawns. But the person for whom you mow the lawn has no bicycles. He pays you with money and you take this to the bicycle shop and buy your bicycle. Money made it possible to exchange your work for something you wanted.

Second, money is a "yardstick of value." This means money may be used to measure and compare the values of various things. You're willing to mow the lawn for an hour for 50 cents. A bicycle costs $25. You now have an idea of the value of a bicycle in terms of your work.

Third, money is a "storehouse of value." You can't store up your crop of tomatoes, because they're perishable. But if you sell them you can store up the money for future use.

Fourth, money serves as a "standard for future payments." You pay $5 down on the bicycle and promise to pay the rest later. You will not pay in eggs or tomatoes or baseballs. You and the bicycle store owner have agreed on exactly what you will pay later. You use money as a form in which later payments can be made.

HOW DID COINS GET THEIR NAMES?

In the world of coins and money there are many fascinating stories of how things came to get their names. Let's consider just a few of them in this column.

We'll start with the word "money" itself. In ancient Roman times, Juno was the goddess of warning. The Romans were so grateful to her for warning them of important dangers, that they put their mint in her temple and made her guardian of the finances. They called her Juno Moneta. "Moneta" came from the Latin word *moneo,* meaning "to warn." Our word "money" is derived from this.

The word "coin" comes from the Latin *cuneus,* which means "wedge." This is because the dies that made pieces of money looked like wedges.

Our "dollar" goes back to the days when money was being coined in Bohemia, where there were silver mines. The mint was located in a place called Joachimsthal, so the coins were called *Joachimsthaler.* In time this became *thaler* and finally "dollar."

Our "dime" comes originally from the Latin word *decimus,* which means "tenth." The "cent" comes directly from the French word *cent,* which means "one hundred," and the Latin *centum.* The idea was that one hundred cents make a dollar.

Our "nickel" is so called because it was made of that metal. The coins of other countries also have interesting histories regarding their names. The English "pound" comes from the Latin *pondo,* which means "pound" as a weight. Originally the full expression was *libra pondo,* or "a pound by weight." By the way, that's where we get our abbreviation for a pound— lb. The Spanish *peso* and Italian *lira* also refer to certain weights.

The French *franc* came from the Latin words *Francorum Rex,* for "King of the Franks," which appeared on their first coins. Peru has a coin called the *sol.* This is the Spanish name for the sun. As you know, the Incas of Peru worshipped the sun long ago!

The words crown, sovereign, *krone, kroon, krona,* and *corona,* all used as names of coins in different countries, show that some crown authority first gave permission to make them. In Panama, the *balboa* is named in honor of the great explorer, and Venezuela has the *bolivar* after its national hero.

HOW DID WE GET OUR SYSTEM OF MEASUREMENT?

Every country in the world has some way of measuring weight, volume, and quantity. This is necessary in order to carry on trade or any form of exchange. But the system of weight and measurement in one country is not always the same as that in another.

Most of the measures we use in the United States came from England and are called "the English system of measures." England and the United States are practically the only countries that use this system today.

The units of measurement in this system have come down to us from ancient times. Most of them grew out of simple, practical ways of measuring. For instance, when people in ancient Rome wanted to measure length, they used the length of a man's foot as a standard. The width of a finger, or the length of the index finger to the first joint, was the origin of the inch!

To measure a yard, people used to take the length of a man's arm. In Rome the length of a thousand paces (a pace was a double step) was used for long distances and became our mile. Of course, this was not a very exact way of measuring. In fact, at one time in the Roman Empire there were 200 different lengths for the foot! And in our own country in Colonial times, the units of measurement were different from colony to colony.

In modern times, it is very important that units of measurement be the same everywhere. So Congress was given the right to fix the standards of weights and measures, and in Washington, D. C., the Bureau of Standards keeps the standard units of measure. For instance, there is a platinum bar, very carefully guarded, which is the standard for measuring length. The correctness of all other measuring units can be checked by comparing them with the standard units in Washington.

If a single international system of weights and measures were to be adopted, it would probably be the metric system. This was worked out in France in 1789, and is used by most countries today. The metric system is based on the meter, which is 39.37 inches. The metric system is based on 10, so each unit of length is 10 times as large as the next smaller unit.

WHEN WERE THE FIRST POLICE ORGANIZED?

The "cop" you see in your town is a rather unique individual in this world! He belongs to a "local" police force. In almost all other countries of the world, the police force is a national organization and is part of the national government. But the United States has the most decentralized (independent) police system in the world. There are town police, city police, county police, and state police!

Police date back to the very earliest history of man. The leader or ruler of a tribe or clan in primitive times depended upon his warriors to keep peace among the people and enforce rules of conduct. The pharaohs of ancient Egypt did the same thing—used their soldiers as police.

About the time of the birth of Christ, Caesar Augustus formed a special police force for the city of Rome, and this lasted for about 350 years. But the job of this police force was still to carry out the imperial orders.

Sometime between the years A.D. 700 and 800, a new idea arose regarding a police force. Instead of carrying out the king's orders against the people, it was felt a police force should enforce the law and protect the people! It was this idea which influenced the development of the police force in England, and later in the United States.

The English developed a system of "watch" and "ward." The watch was a night guard and the ward a day guard for the local area. The colonists brought this system to the United States. They had the night watch under constables, with all able-bodied men over 16 serving without pay. Most cities and towns used this system well into the 1800's.

The use of daytime police started in Boston in 1838 with a force of six men. Then two states passed laws—New York in 1845 and Pennsylvania in 1856—that became the basis for setting up the modern police forces in the United States. The early policemen often didn't wear uniforms or badges! But finally, in 1856, New York City police adopted full police uniforms, and soon other cities followed this idea.

WHAT IS THE F.B.I.?

The F.B.I. is one of the best-known and most "glamorous" departments of the Federal Government. Its full name is the Federal Bureau of Investigation, and it was founded in 1908 as a bureau within the United States Department of Justice.

The F.B.I. has authority to investigate violations of Federal laws and matters in which the United States is, or may be, a party in interest. In 1924, the Identification Division of the F.B.I. was created. It started with a library of 810,188 fingerprint records. Today, the F.B.I. has the fingerprint cards of more than 100,000,000 people!

The headquarters of the F.B.I. are in Washington, D.C. Along with its own responsibilities, the F.B.I. is a service organization for local law enforcement agencies. Its facilities are available for the assistance of municipal, county, and state police departments.

The Identification Division serves as the central clearing house for fingerprints and criminal data. When a person is arrested and his fingerprints are sent to the F.B.I., it can be determined in less than five minutes whether he has a previous criminal record. A copy of this record is sent to the interested law enforcement agency within 36 hours after the card is received in Washington.

The facilities of the F.B.I. laboratory are likewise available to all law enforcement agencies. Provided with the most modern equipment, its scientists are daily making examinations of documents, blood, hair, soil, and other types of matter. When evidence in a local case has been examined, F.B.I. experts will testify concerning their findings in the state court.

In June, 1939, the President of the United States selected the F.B.I. as the agency responsible for the investigation of espionage, sabotage, and other national defense matters.

HOW DID FINGERPRINTING START?

Man has known for a long time that the ridges of his fingertips formed certain patterns. In fact, the Chinese have used fingerprints for hundreds of years in various forms and for various purposes.

But the value of fingerprints in detecting criminals was realized by science only in quite recent years. The first man to suggest that fingerprints be used to identify criminals was Dr. Henry Faulds of England in 1880. In 1892, Sir Francis Galton, a noted English scientist, scientifically established the fact that no two fingerprints were alike. He was the first one to set up a collection of fingerprint records.

The British Government became interested in his theories and ordered a commission to study the idea of using a fingerprint system in the identification of criminals. One of the members of this commission, Sir Edward Henry, later became head of Scotland Yard.

Sir Henry devised a system of classifying and filing fingerprints. You can understand that without such a system it would take very long to match up two sets of fingerprints, and in crime detection, speed is often very important.

According to Sir Henry's system, all finger impressions are divided into the following types of patterns: loops, central pocket loops, double loops, arches, tented arches, whorls, and accidentals. By counting the ridges between the fixed points in the pattern, it is possible to classify each of the 10 fingers into a definite group. The 10 fingers are then considered as a unit to obtain the complete classification. With this system, fingerprints are filed in a sequence, without reference to name, description, or crime speciality of the individual. An office can contain millions of prints, and yet identification can be established in a few minutes!

The FBI file of more than 100,000,000 fingerprint cards include fingerprints from many persons who want some means of identification in case of sickness. It also includes fingerprints of those in the Armed Services and Government employees.

Today, all aliens have to be fingerprinted, and many industries vital to the national defense require fingerprinting of their employees.

HOW DID MEDICINE BEGIN?

Medicine is the treating of disease. Now, you yourself know that there are many ways to treat disease. If someone in your family gets sick, you could call a doctor and he would apply all his knowledge and skill. He would treat the disease scientifically. But you might instead depend on some "remedy" your grandmother knew, or try to cure the person by saying some "magic" words. You would then be treating the disease unscientifically.

The history of medicine includes the prescientific stage, before it was a science, and the time when it became a science. The medicine of primitive peoples had all kinds of strange explanations of disease. And in treating disease, primitive medicine depended on magic or on anything that seemed to work. But surprisingly enough, medicine among primitive people included application of heat and cold, bloodletting, massage, the use of herbs.

Ancient Egyptian medicine, which was the best-known medicine before the scientific, depended chiefly on magic. It used all kinds of ointments and potions. Among the "drugs" it used were honey, salt, cedar oil, the brain, liver, heart, and blood of various animals. Sometimes this prescientific medicine seemed to work, sometimes it didn't.

But it wasn't until the time of the Greeks that scientific medicine began. More than two thousand years ago, a man called Hippocrates put together a collection of medical books, "The Hippocratic Collection." It was the beginning of scientific medicine because it depended on close observation of patients for learning about diseases.

In these books there were records of actual cases and what had happened to the patients. For the first time, instead of depending on some magic formula, treatment was given as the result of studying the patient and the disease and applying past experience. In this way modern medicine was born.

WHEN DID PEOPLE START CUTTING THEIR HAIR?

The hair is actually a development of the horn layer of the skin. Like our nails, it doesn't hurt us to cut it because these horn cells contain no nerves. Because the hair is such an important part of our appearance and because it is so easy to cut and arrange in almost any fashion, men and women have been "doing things" with their hair since the beginning of time.

No one can say who first thought of cutting the hair or arranging it in a special way. We know that women have had combs from the very earliest times, thousands of years ago! Men and women have also curled their hair since ancient times.

But the custom of long hair for women and short hair for men is more modern. During the Middle Ages men wore their hair long, curled it, even wore it with ribbons! If the hair wasn't long enough, they wore false hair bought from country people.

Henry VIII of England began the style of short hair for men. He ordered all men to wear their hair short but allowed them to grow beards and curl their moustaches. When James I became King, long hair for men reappeared, including wigs.

About the middle of the 17th century, there were two camps in England when it came to hair: those who believed in short hair and long beards for men, and those who believed in short beards and long hair. For the next hundred years the custom changed back and forth. Finally, about 1800, the custom became definitely established for men to wear their hair short.

Women have always tended to wear long hair, but bobbing the hair was a fad at the Court of Louis XIV! Today, of course, women wear their hair short not only because it is fashionable, but because it is simpler than having to bother with pins and combs and elaborate coifs.

Barbers and barber shops are a fairly recent development, too. In England, barbers were first incorporated as a craft in 1461, and in France, during the reign of Louis XIV.

WHEN WAS SOAP FIRST MADE?

You might think that something as useful and necessary as soap had been one of the first inventions of man. But soap is quite a modern thing in man's history. It only goes back about 2,000 years.

What ancient peoples used to do was to anoint their bodies with olive oil. They also used the juices and ashes of various plants to clean themselves. But by the time of Pliny (a Roman writer of the first century A.D.) we already have a reference to two kinds of soap, soft and hard. He describes it as an invention for brightening up the hair and gives the Gauls credit for inventing it.

By the way, in the ruins of Pompeii, there was found buried an establishment for turning out soap that very much resembles the soap of today! And yet, just one hundred years ago, nearly all the soap used in the United States was made at home!

Soap is made by boiling fats and oils with an alkali. In the great soap factories, the fats and alkalis are first boiled in huge kettles. This process is called "saponification." When it is nearly completed, salt is added. This causes the soap to rise to the top of the kettle. The brine or salt solution containing glycerine, dirt, and some excess alkali sinks to the bottom and is drawn off. This process may be repeated as many as five or six times. More water and alkali are added each time until the last bit of fat is saponified, or converted from a fat into soap.

The next step is to churn the soap into a smooth mass while adding various ingredients, such as perfumes, coloring matter, water softeners, and preservatives. After this, the hot melted soap is ready to be fashioned into bars or cakes, or granules, flakes, or globules. Toilet soaps go through a process called "milling," which shreds and dries them, then rolls them into sheets.

WHO INVENTED SHOES?

When primitive man had to make his way over rocks, he discovered the need for covering his feet to protect them. So the first shoes, which were probably sandals, were mats of grass, strips of hide, or even flat pieces of wood.

These were fastened to the soles of the feet by thongs that were then bound around the ankles. Of course, in colder regions, these sandals didn't protect the feet sufficiently, so more material was added and gradually the sandals developed into shoes.

Among the first civilized people to make shoes were the Egyptians. They used pads of leather or papyrus, which were bound to the foot by two straps. In order to protect the toes, the front of the sandal was sometimes turned up.

The Romans went a step further and developed a kind of shoe called the *calceus*. This had slits at the side and straps knotted in front. There were different forms of the *calceus,* to be worn by the different classes of society.

In some of the cold regions of the earth, people developed a kind of shoe independently. For example, they sometimes wore bags padded with grass and tied around the feet. In time, these first foot coverings developed into the moccasins of the Eskimo and the Indian.

As far as our modern shoes are concerned, their beginnings can be traced to the Crusades. The Crusaders went on long pilgrimages, and they needed protection for their feet, so it became necessary to create shoes that would last a long time. In time, leather shoes of great beauty began to appear in Italy, France, and England.

Shoes have always been subject to whims of fashion. For example, at the time of King James I of England, high heels and very soft leathers were fashionable in society. It made for difficult walking, but people insisted on wearing them. At one time, before the appearance of the high heel, long-toed shoes were considered fashionable. The shoes were very narrow, and the toes were five and six inches long, coming to a point. Shoemaking was introduced into the United States in 1629, when Thomas Beard arrived under contract to make shoes for the Pilgrim colony.

WHO MADE THE FIRST FALSE TEETH?

Nobody looks good when he has some teeth missing. Besides, it sometimes interferes very seriously with eating and chewing. So man decided long ago that when he lost his natural teeth for one reason or another, they should be replaced. Substituting artificial replacements for natural parts in teeth is called "prosthetics."

When the natural teeth are gone, they are replaced either by bridgework or by dentures. In bridgework, the "load" of false teeth is borne by our natural teeth on either side of the gap. The bridge fits on these natural teeth. In a denture, the false teeth are held in place by resting on the gum and other parts of the mouth under the gum.

It may amaze you to learn that bridges with false teeth were made

3,000 years ago by the Etruscans, who worked with gold! Dentures, including "complete" dentures for people who had no teeth left, have been made for about 300 years.

The first problems to be solved in making both bridges and dentures was how to make them stay in the mouth in the right position, and how to make the "baseplate material," the material that held the false teeth. Modern dentistry has solved both these problems so well that people with false teeth can eat and chew as well as anyone, and the false teeth feel light and natural in the mouth.

But what about the teeth themselves? In early times, false teeth were made from bone, ivory, and hippopotamus tooth! Sometimes the entire bridge or denture was carved from the same material, and it was all one piece that fitted into the mouth. Later on, individual human teeth, or the teeth of various animals, especially the sheep, were used. These were mounted on a gold or ivory base.

At the end of the 18th century, teeth were made of porcelain, and soon individual porcelain teeth were mounted on gold or platinum bases. The materials in making teeth are the same as those used in making other fine porcelain. They have a fine texture, are somewhat translucent, and have great strength.

About 100 years ago false teeth began to be designed to harmonize with the shape of the face. Today, false teeth are matched to natural teeth so closely in color and shape that it is hard to tell them apart!

HOW DID FORKS ORIGINATE?

The first man to use a crude kind of fork for eating probably lived thousands of years ago. But the everyday use of forks in dining is a very recent development in the history of man.

The primitive savage used a small pronged twig as a kind of natural fork to pick up his meat. Some authorities believe that the fork really originated with the arrow, and that at first it was a kind of toothpick used to remove food from between the teeth.

Actual forks as we know them were first used only for cooking and for holding the meat while it was being carved. These first forks were long, and two-pronged, and were made of iron, bone, and hard wood.

It took a very long time for forks to be accepted in general use in dining.

Only 300 years ago, forks were great curiosities in Europe. In fact, in France everyone ate with his fingers until the 17th century. We all know about the magnificent Court of Louis XIV and the great banquets at his palaces. Did you know that no one used a fork at this very elegant Court!

When people first began to use forks for eating, other people used to ridicule them as being too dainty. When a rich woman in Venice in the 11th century had a small golden fork made, it was written about her: "Instead of eating like other people, she had her food cut up into little pieces, and ate the pieces by means of a two-pronged fork."

Five hundred years later, in the 16th century, people who used forks in Venice were still being described as somewhat peculiar: "At Venice each person is served, besides his knife and spoon, with a fork to hold the meat while he cuts it, for they deem it ill manners that one should touch it with his hand."

From the 17th century on, table manners developed along modern lines. Silver forks began to appear all over Italy. And by the end of the 18th century, the fork was accepted as a necessity in the homes of most cultivated people.

WHEN DID MAN BEGIN TO DRINK MILK?

Today, when we say "milk" we usually mean cows' milk, since most milk consumed by human beings is from the cow. But milk from other animals is consumed by people all over the world. Half the milk consumed in India is from the buffalo. Goats' milk is widely used in countries along the Mediterranean, and the milk of reindeer is used as food in Northern Europe.

When did man first begin to drink the milk of animals, and use milk products such as butter and cheese? No one can ever know, since it was before recorded history. Soured milks, butterlike products, and cheese were probably common foods of the people roaming the grasslands of Asia with their sheep and cattle thousands of years ago.

The Bible has many references to milk. Abel, son of Adam, was a "keeper of sheep" and probably consumed milk. The earliest mention of milk in the Bible is Jacob's prediction in 1700 B.C. that Judah's teeth shall be "white with milk." Canaan was "a land of milk and honey" in 1500 B.C. Job also refers to cheese. But in all these cases the mention of milk implies that it was used much earlier.

We may think that the idea of making concentrated and dry milk is a modern one. Actually, the Tatars prepared concentrated milks in paste, and probably in dry form as early as the year 1200 and used them as food during the raids under Genghis Khan.

The original patent for evaporated milk was granted in 1856, and this type of milk was widely used by soldiers in the Civil War.

About 87 per cent of the milk from the cow is water, but the remainder supplies man with a high percentage of his daily requirements in calcium, protein, and vitamins A and B.

WHERE DID ICE CREAM ORIGINATE?

The way we eat ice cream in this country—more than 2,000,000,000 quarts of it each year!—you'd imagine that it originated in the United States.

But the fact is the ice cream was first created in the Orient. The great Venetian explorer Marco Polo saw people eating it there and brought back the idea to Italy. From Italy the idea was carried to France. It became very popular in France with the nobility and an effort was made to keep the recipes for ice cream a secret from the common people. But, of course, they soon learned how delicious this new food was and ice cream became popular with everyone. Soon it spread all over the world, including the United States.

The first wholesale factory for the manufacture of ice cream was started in Baltimore, Maryland, in 1851. The real development of ice cream and the ice cream business didn't take place until after 1900 with new developments in refrigeration.

The basis of all ice cream is cream, milk or milk solids, sugar, and sometimes eggs. Vanilla, chocolate, berries, fruit ingredients, and nuts are added as flavors. This is the usual proportion of ingredients in ice cream: about 80 to 85 per cent cream and milk products, 15 per cent sugar, one-half to four and one-half per cent flavoring, and three-tenths of one per cent stabilizer.

The small amount of stabilizer is used in order to retain the smoothness of the ice cream by preventing the formation of coarse ice crystals. Pure food gelatine is usually used for this purpose.

When you eat one-third of a pint of vanilla ice cream you are getting about as much calcium, protein, and the B vitamins as are in one-half cup of whole milk, and as much vitamin A and calories as in one cup of milk.

HOW DID CANDY ORIGINATE?

In almost every country in ancient times people ate something that was like candy. In excavations in Egypt, pictures and written records have been found that showed candy and how candy in Egypt was made!

In those days, of course, the refining of sugar was unknown, so honey was used as a sweetener. The chief ingredient of the candy in Egypt was dates.

In parts of the East, each tribe had its official candy-maker and secret recipes. In these regions, almonds, honey, and figs have long been used in making candy. There is an ancient Roman recipe that directs nut meats and cooked poppy be boiled with honey, then peppered and sprinkled with ground sesame softened with honey. The result would probably be a sort of nougat.

In Europe, they had sweet sirup in early times, but it was used to hide the taste of medicines. No one thought of making candy for its own sake. But when large quantities of sugar from the Colonies began to appear in Europe in the 17th century, candy-making began to be a separate art.

The French candied fruits and developed other recipes. One of these, a nut- and sugar-sirup sweetmeat called "prawlings," may have been the ancestor of the famous New Orleans pralines.

In Colonial days and later, maple sugar, molasses, and honey were used in homemade sweetmeats. Our great-grandmothers candied iris root and ginger "varnished" apples, and made rock candy.

The main ingredients used for the manufacturing of candy are cane and beet sugars combined with corn sirup, corn sugar, corn starch, honey, molasses, and maple sugar. To this sweet base are added chocolate, fruits, nuts, eggs, milk, a variety of milk products, and, of course, flavors and colors. Some flavors are from natural sources, such as vanilla, peppermint, lemon, and so on, and others are imitations of true flavors.

There are more than 2,000 different kinds of candy being made today. In the United States more than 2,500,000,000 pounds are produced every year!

HOW WAS FIRE DISCOVERED?

Fire has been known to man since the very earliest times. In certain caves in Europe in which men lived hundreds of thousands of years ago, charcoal and charred bits of bone have been found among stones that were evidently used as fireplaces.

But how did men learn the trick of making a fire? We can only guess. Early man probably knew how to use fire before he knew how to start it. For example, lightning might strike a rotten tree and the trunk would smolder. From this he would light a fire and keep it going for years.

We can take a pretty good guess as to how the cave men learned to start a fire. In trampling among the loose stones in the dark, the first men must have noticed sparks when one stone struck another. But it may have taken many generations before anyone among these early men had the idea of purposely striking two stones together to produce a fire!

Another way we have of knowing how early men discovered fire is to observe the primitive people of today. Some of them are in a stage of development that our forefathers reached thousands of years ago.

Let's look at some of these primitive methods. In Alaska, Indians of certain tribes rub sulphur over two stones and strike them together. When the sulphur ignites, they drop the burning stone among some dried grass or other material.

In China and India, a piece of broken pottery is struck against a bamboo stick. The outer coating of the bamboo is very hard and seems to have the qualities of flint. The Eskimos strike a common piece of quartz against a piece of iron pyrites, which is very common where they live. Among the North American Indians, rubbing two sticks together to produce fire was a common method.

The ancient Greeks and Romans had still another method. They used a kind of lens, called "a burning glass," to focus the rays of the sun. When the heat rays were concentrated in this way, they were hot enough to set fire to dry wood.

An interesting thing about fire in early days, is that many ancient peoples kept "perpetual" fires going. The Mayas and Aztecs in Mexico kept a fire perpetually burning, and the Greeks, Egyptians, and Romans kept fires burning in their temples.

WHO INVENTED MATCHES?

Man's desire to be able to start a fire to warm himself and cook food has caused him to invent a variety of "matches." The cave man struck a spark from a flint and hoped it would ignite some dry leaves. The Romans, thousands of years later, were not much further advanced. They struck two flinty stones together and caught the spark on a split of wood covered with sulphur.

During the Middle Ages, sparks struck by flint and steel were caught on charred rags, dried moss, or fungus. Such material that catches fire easily is called "tinder."

Modern matches were made possible by the discovery of phosphorus, a substance which catches fire at a very low temperature. In 1681, an Englishman called Robert Boyle dipped a sliver of wood which had been treated with sulphur into a mixture of sulphur and phosphorus. But the matches took fire so easily that his invention wasn't practical.

The first practical matches were made in England by a druggist named John Walker. In order to light them, they were drawn between folds of paper covered with ground glass. By 1833, phosphorus-tipped matches that could be ignited by friction were being made in Austria and Germany. But there was one problem. White or yellow phosphorus was so dangerous to the match-workers that it had to be forbidden by an international treaty in 1906.

Finally, a non-poisonous red phosphorus was introduced, and this led to the invention of safety matches. The first safety matches, which light only on a prepared surface, were made in Sweden in 1844. Instead of putting all the necessary chemicals in the match-head, the red phosphorus was painted into the striking surface on the container. The match was thus "safe" unless it was rubbed on the striking area.

During World War II our troops were fighting in the Pacific tropics where long rainy periods made ordinary matches ineffective. A man called Raymond Cady invented a coating for matches which kept them efficient even after eight hours under water!

WHO DISCOVERED ELECTRICITY?

The curious thing about electricity is that it has been studied for thousands of years—and we still don't know exactly what it is! Today, all matter is thought to consist of tiny charged particles. Electricity, according to this theory, is simply a moving stream of electrons or other charged particles.

The word "electricity" comes from the Greek word *electron*. And do you know what this word meant? It was the Greek word for "amber"! You see, as far back as 600 B.C. the Greeks knew that when amber was rubbed, it became capable of attracting to it light bits of cork or paper.

Not much progress was made in the study of electricity until 1672. In that year, a man called Otto von Guericke produced a more powerful charge of electricity by holding his hand against a ball of spinning sulphur. In 1729, Stephen Gray found that some substances, such as metals, carried electricity from one location to another. These came to be called "conductors." He found that others, such as glass, sulphur, amber, and wax, did not carry electricity. These were called "insulators."

The next important step took place in 1733 when a Frenchman called du Fay discovered positive and negative charges of electricity, although he thought these were two different kinds of electricity.

But it was Benjamin Franklin who tried to give an explanation of what electricity was. His idea was that all substances in nature contain "electrical fluid." Friction between certain substances removed some of this "fluid" from one and placed an extra amount in the other. Today, we would say that this "fluid" is composed of electrons which are negatively charged.

Probably the most important developments in the science of electricity started with the invention of the first battery in 1800 by Alessandro Volta. This battery gave the world its first continuous, reliable source of electric current, and led to all the important discoveries of the use of electricity.

WHEN WERE ROCKETS FIRST USED?

Have you ever watched a lawn sprinkler work—the kind that spins around and around and sprays water in a circle? Well, you were actually watching the principle of the rocket at work!

The water in the sprinkler was escaping in one direction. This force pushed the sprinkler in the opposite direction. In a rocket, a fast-burning fuel or explosive exerts force in one direction, and this pushes the rocket forward in the opposite direction.

We think of ourselves as living in the age of rockets, and of rockets as being a rather modern invention. But rockets are a very old idea. The Chinese invented them and used them as fireworks more than 800 years ago! They then became known in Indian and Arabian countries. The first record of them in Western Europe was in A.D. 1256.

The first use of rockets in war was very similar to the way burning arrows had been used. They were aimed at homes to set them on fire. Soldiers and sailors continued to use rockets as signals, but they were no longer used for war for a long time.

In 1802, a British Army captain read how British troops in India had been attacked with rockets. This gave him the idea of trying them out with the British Army. The experiment was so successful that very soon most European armies as well as the Army of the United States began to use war rockets.

In Europe, rockets were used in the Battle of Leipzig, in which Napoleon was defeated. In the United States, the English used war rockets in the bombardment of Fort McHenry in Baltimore Harbor. This is why in the national anthem of the United States there is the phrase, "the rocket's red glare!"

During the 19th century, as artillery became more powerful and more accurate, it began to replace rockets, and they were not important in war again until World War II and the famous German V-2 rocket.

HOW WAS GLASS DISCOVERED?

For thousands of years glass was thought of as something to look at. It was valued for decoration and for making precious objects. Glass really became useful when it was thought of as something to look through.

No one really knows when or where the secret of making glass was first learned, though we know it has been used since very early days. The chief ingredients for making glass are sand, soda ash, or potash and lime, melted together at a high temperature. Since these materials are found in abundance in many parts of the world, the secret of glassmaking could have been discovered in many countries.

According to one story, the ancient Phoenicians deserve the credit for this discovery. A crew of a ship landed at the mouth of a river in Syria. When they were ready to cook their dinner, they could find no stones on which to support their kettle. So they used lumps of niter (a sodium compound) from the ship's cargo. The heat of the fire melted the niter, which mixed with the surrounding sand and flowed out as a stream of liquid glass!

This story may or may not be true, but Syria was one of the original homes of glassmaking. And ancient Phoenician traders sold glassware all through the Mediterranean countries.

Egypt was another country in which glassmaking was known at an early time. Glass beads and charms have been found in tombs which date back as far as 7000 B.C., but these glass objects may have come from Syria. We know that about 1500 B.C. the Egyptians were making their own glass.

The Egyptians mixed crushed quartz pebbles with the sand to change the color of the glass. They learned, too, that by adding cobalt, copper, or manganese to the mixture, they could produce glass with rich blue, green, or purple color.

After 1200 B.C. the Egyptians learned to press glass into molds. But the blowpipe for blowing glass did not come into use until shortly before the beginning of the Christian Era. It was a Phoenician invention.

The Romans were great glassmakers, and even used glass in thin panes as a coating for walls. By the time of the Christian Era, glass was already being used for windowpanes!

WHO INVENTED THE THERMOMETER?

Do you ever find yourself asking: I wonder how hot it is? Or: I wonder how cold this is? If you are interested in heat, just imagine all the questions about heat that scientists want to know! But the first step in developing the science of heat is to have some way of measuring it. And that's why the thermometer was invented. "Thermo" means "heat," and "meter" means "measure," so a thermometer measures heat.

The first condition about having a thermometer must be that it will always give the same indication at the same temperature. With this in mind, an Italian scientist called Galileo began certain experiments around 1592 (100 years after Columbus discovered America). He made a kind of thermometer which is really called "an air thermoscope." He had a glass tube with a hollow bulb at one end. In this tube there was air. The tube and bulb were heated to expand the air inside, and then the open end was placed in a fluid, such as water.

As the air in the tube cooled, its volume contracted or shrank, and the liquid rose in the tube to take its place. Changes in temperature could then be noted by the rising or falling level of the liquid in the tube. So here we have the first "thermometer" because it measures heat. But remember, it measures heat by measuring the expansion and contraction of air in a tube. So it was discovered that one of the problems with this thermometer was that it was affected by variations of atmospheric pressure, and therefore, wasn't completely accurate.

The type of thermometer we use today uses the expansion and contraction of a liquid to measure temperature. This liquid is hermetically sealed in a glass bulb with a fine tube attached. Higher temperature makes the liquid expand and go up the tube, lower temperature makes the liquid contract and drop in the tube. A scale on the tube tells us the temperature.

This kind of thermometer was first used about 1654 by the Grand Duke Ferdinand II of Tuscany.

WHO INVENTED THE MICROSCOPE?

The word microscope is a combination of two Greek words, *mikros,* or "small," and *skopos,* or "watcher." So a microscope is a "watcher of the small"! It is an instrument used to see tiny things which are invisible to the naked eye.

Normally an object appears larger the closer it is brought to the human eye. But when it is nearer than 10 inches, it is no longer clear. It is said to be out of focus. Now if a simple convex lens is placed between the eye and the object, the object can be brought nearer than 10 inches and still remain in focus.

Today we describe this simply as "using a magnifying glass." But ordinary magnifying glasses are really "simple microscopes," and as such they have been known since remote times. So when we speak of the invention of the microscope, we really mean "the compound microscope." In fact, today when we say "microscope," that's the only kind we mean.

What is a compound microscope? In this kind of microscope, magnification takes place in two stages. There is a lens called "the objective" which produces a primary magnified image. Then there is another lens called "the eyepiece" or "ocular," which magnifies that first image. In actual practice, there are several lenses used for both the objective and ocular, but the principle is that of two-stage magnification.

The compound microscope was invented some time between 1590 and 1610. While no one is quite sure who actually did it, the credit is usually given to Galileo. A Dutch scientist called Leeuwenhoek is sometimes called "the father of the microscope," but that's because of the many discoveries he made with the microscope.

Leeuwenhoek showed that weevils, fleas, and other minute creatures come from eggs and are not "spontaneously generated." He was the first to see such microscopic forms of life as the protozoa and bacteria. With his own microscope he was the first to see the whole circulation of the blood.

Today the microscope is important to man in almost every form of science and industry.

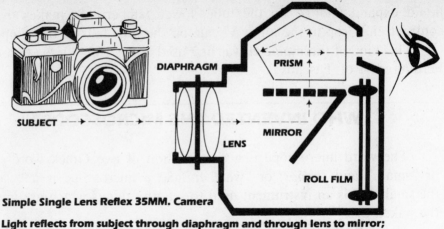

Simple Single Lens Reflex 35MM. Camera

Light reflects from subject through diaphragm and through lens to mirror;
then to prism in reflex housing to viewer's eye. When shutter release is
pressed, mirror lifts out of way so that light will expose the film.

WHO INVENTED THE CAMERA?

Today, when you snap a picture and have it developed so easily, it's hard to believe that hundreds of years of experimenting were needed before this became possible. Photography was not invented by any single person. Just to give you an idea of what went into bringing it to its present stage of perfection, here is a quick outline of the history of photography.

Between the 11th and 16th centuries, man had "the camera obscura." This enabled him to show on paper an image which could be traced by hand to give accurate drawings of natural scenes. It didn't really "take" a picture.

In 1568, Daniello Barbaro fitted the camera obscura with a lens and a changeable opening to sharpen the image. In 1802, Thomas Wedgwood and Sir Humphrey Davy recorded silhouettes and images of paintings on coated paper by contact printing, but they couldn't make the prints permanent.

In 1816, Joseph Niepce made a crude photographic camera from a jewel box and a lens taken from a microscope. He was able to make a negative image. In 1835, William Talbot was the first to make positives from negatives, the first to make permanent images.

In 1839, Louis Daguerre announced the daguerreotype process, which recorded the image on a silver plate. More and more developments were contributed by individuals all over the world as time went on. Many of them are too technical to discuss here, but as you can see, it was a long slow process of growth.

Finally, in 1888, a box camera was put on the market, developed by the Eastman Dry Plate and Film Company, using the Kodak system. The camera was sold already loaded with enough film for 100 exposures. The pictures were 2½-inch-diameter size. After exposure, camera and film were returned to Rochester, where the film was removed and processed and the camera reloaded and returned to the customer.

This box camera was probably the beginning of popular photography as we know it today when billions of pictures are taken every year by people all over the world.

WHO INVENTED THE AUTOMOBILE?

Unlike so many other great developments, no one man can claim credit for inventing the automobile. It has reached its present state of perfection as the result of a great many ideas contributed through the years.

For all practical purposes, the first land vehicle that was self-propelled with an engine was built in 1769 by a Frenchman named Nicholas Cugnot. It was a cumbersome three-wheeled cart with a steam engine and an enormous boiler. It could travel 3 miles an hour and had to be refueled every 15 miles!

In 1789, an American called Oliver Evans received the first United States patent for a self-propelled carriage. It was a four-wheeled wagon and had a paddle wheel at the rear so that it could operate either on land or in the water. It weighed 21 tons!

For nearly 80 years afterward, other men continued to experiment with powered carriages for use on roads. Most of them were steam, although a few were electrically driven and had to carry large batteries. Then, in the 1880's came two inventions that were to result in the automobile as we know it today. One was the development of the gasoline engine. The other was the invention of the pneumatic, or air-filled, tire.

The first gasoline-powered car was put on the road in 1887 by Gottlieb Daimler, a German. In the United States, two brothers, Frank and Charles Duryea, built the first successful American gasoline automobile in 1892 or 1893. Their machine was described as "a horseless buggy." As a matter of fact, all the early American automobiles that were to follow were really buggies! Nobody attempted to design a completely different kind of vehicle. All they did was add a gasoline engine to the buggies and a connecting belt or chain to drive the rear wheels.

It was only after automobiles began to run successfully that attention was turned to making them comfortable and stronger. Car-makers soon found that the flimsy construction of buggies was not suitable for use in automobiles. Gradually, the familiar form of the automobile as we know it today began to emerge. Engines were removed from under the seats and placed in front. Stronger wheels replaced the spindly bicycle and carriage wheels. Steering wheels replaced "tillers." Finally, steel was used instead of wood to make stronger frames and our modern automobile became a reality.

WHO INVENTED THE AIRPLANE?

Sometimes an invention starts with having the "idea." A man has the idea that people might want a certain kind of machine or product, and then he proceeds to "invent" it.

But when it comes to the airplane, the "idea" has been one of man's oldest dreams. The idea of flying has fascinated men since ancient days. In fact, one of our most famous legends tells of Icarus, who fastened wings to his body with wax and flew off! As he soared toward the sun, however, the wax melted and he fell to his death. Icarus is a symbol of man's striving to new heights.

Leonardo da Vinci, who was also quite an inventor, made sketches of a flying machine that used manpower, and other artists and "dreamers" had the idea of an airplane hundreds of years ago.

The earliest flying machines that were made had no power. They were actually huge kites or gliders, and during the 19th century many experiments with these were carried on.

But nobody had yet made a heavier-than-air machine that was equipped with its own power. In fact, there was some question that such a machine could actually be built. The first man to demonstrate that it could be done was Professor Samuel Langley, who was secretary of the Smithsonian Institution of Washington, D.C. He built two machines, each about 12 feet wide and 15 feet long, driven by 1½-horsepower steam engines. In 1896, these two models made successful flights. In 1903, when Langley's full-sized flying machine was tested, it was wrecked. This was on October 7, 1903.

On December 17, Orville and Wilbur Wright succeeded in making man's first flight in a heavier-than-air machine with its own power. At Kitty

Hawk, North Carolina, they made one flight of 120 feet in 12 seconds, and a second flight of 852 feet in 59 seconds. The airplane was born!

HOW WAS THE TELEPHONE INVENTED?

The story of the invention of the telephone is a very dramatic one. (No wonder they were able to make a movie about it!) But first let's make sure we understand the principle of how a telephone works.

When you speak, the air makes your vocal cords vibrate. These vibrations are passed on to the air molecules so that sound waves come out of your mouth, that is, vibrations in the air. These sound waves strike an aluminum disk or diaphragm in the transmitter of your telephone. And the disk vibrates back and forth in just the same way the molecules of air are vibrating.

These vibrations send a varying, or undulating, current over the telephone line. The weaker and stronger currents cause a disk in the receiver at the other end of the line to vibrate exactly as the diaphragm in the transmitter is vibrating. This sets up waves in the air exactly like those which you sent into the mouthpiece. When these sound waves reach the ear of the person at the other end, they have the same effect as they would have if they came directly from your mouth!

Now to the story of Alexander Graham Bell and how he invented the telephone. On June 2, 1875, he was experimenting in Boston with the idea of sending several telegraph messages over the same wire at the same time. He was using a set of spring-steel reeds. He was working with the receiving set in one room, while his assistant, Thomas Watson, operated the sending set in the other room.

Watson plucked a steel reed to make it vibrate, and it produced a twanging sound. Suddenly Bell came rushing in, crying to Watson: "Don't change anything. What did you do then? Let me see." He found that the steel rod, while vibrating over the magnet, had caused a current of varying strength to flow through the wire. This made the reed in Bell's room vibrate and produce a twanging sound.

The next day the first telephone was made and voice sounds could be recognized over the first telephone line, which was from the top of the building down two flights. Then, on March 10 of next year, the first sentence was heard: "Mr. Watson, come here, I want you."

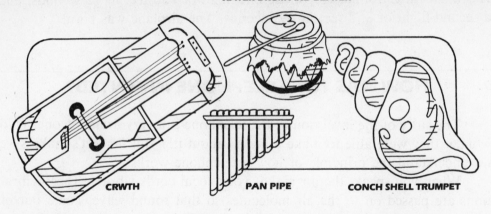

CRWTH   PAN PIPE   CONCH SHELL TRUMPET

WHAT WAS THE FIRST MUSICAL INSTRUMENT?

There is a legend about this, but it is pure fancy. According to a Greek myth, Pan invented the first musical instrument—the shepherd's pipe. One day he sighed through the reeds on a river bank and heard his breath produce a mournful wail as it passed through them. He broke them off in unequal lengths, bound them together, and had the first musical instrument!

The fact is we can never trace the first musical instrument because all primitive people all over the world seem to have made music of some sort. It was usually music that had some religious significance and it was shared in by the spectators who would dance, drum, or clap hands and sing with the music. It was done more than for pleasure alone. This primitive music had a meaning as part of the lives of the people.

The legend of Pan and the reeds suggests, however, how man first had the idea for making various musical instruments. He may have imitated the sounds of nature, or used articles of nature all about him to create his music.

The first instruments were of the drum type. Later, man invented wind instruments, made from the horns of animals. From these crude wind instruments developed modern brass instruments. As man trained his musical sense, he began to use reeds and thus produced more natural tones of greater delicacy.

Last of all, man discovered the use of strings and invented the simple lyre and harp from which developed the instruments played with a bow.

In the Middle Ages, the Crusaders brought back many curious oriental instruments. These, combined with the folk instruments that already existed in Europe, developed into many of the instruments now in use.

HOW DID BASKETBALL GET ITS NAME?

If you had to name the game that is watched by more spectators in the United States than any other, which would it be? Surprisingly enough, it is basketball.

Basketball is often called "the international game" because it is played in every civilized nation of the world. Yet basketball did not develop slowly over the centuries, as some of our other games have. It was invented by one man, James A. Naismith, in 1891.

Naismith wanted to provide a game to interest students of physical education at the Springfield Training School, Springfield, Massachusetts. Naismith was a Canadian and he combined the Indian game of lacrosse and the British game of soccer to make a suitable indoor game.

Instead of using a stick as in lacrosse, or kicking a ball with the foot as in soccer, Naismith devised a game by which the ball is passed from player to player, or bounced (the dribble) by a single player and shot into a goal. When he first created the game, the only thing he had to use for a goal was a wooden peach basket, so he called the game "basketball"!

In basketball, as in many other games, the special talent of a player determines what position he is chosen to play. Those who are good at scoring goals by throwing the ball through the hoop are usually stationed at forward, where they lead the team's attack on the opponents' goal.

The center is usually tall. He should be able to tip the ball to a teammate during the center jump. His height should also give his team "control of the backboard," which means being able to regain control of the ball when a shot fails to go through the hoop. The guards have to keep the opposing forwards from scoring, so they have to be agile, tricky, and able to take their part in offensive passing and shooting.

WHEN DID BOXING BEGIN?

Many people say that boxing should be outlawed. In the history of boxing this has happened many times. People have felt boxing was too cruel or barbaric, and have wanted it stopped.

Imagine how they would feel if they could see the first boxing bouts that were held! These were in ancient Greece, and the boxers performed at Olympic games and other public games. Some of the rules they observed were very much like the ones we have today. But there was one big difference: Instead of gloves, the fighters wore the *cestus*. This was a wrapping of leather studded with lead or bronze plates. A blow from a *cestus,* as you can see, could be quite damaging!

After the fall of the Roman Empire, boxing disappeared, not to reappear until it was revived in England at the beginning of the 18th century. It soon became quite a fashionable sport, and it remained so for more than 100 years.

The fights were decided with bare fists, and many of them lasted for several hours. Wrestling and throwing were allowed. A round ended only when a man was knocked down, and the time between rounds varied. This tough fight went on and on until one of the fighters was unable to walk up to a chalk mark at the center of the ring when a round began!

Naturally, this kind of brutal boxing eventually turned public opinion against prize fighting. Something had to be done to save the sport, so padded gloves began to be used. Then little by little, the old rules were made more humane. Finally, in 1867, came the big step that brought boxing back into favor. The Marquis of Queensberry introduced a set of rules that made many improvements. For example, the rounds were limited to three minutes each. The interval between rounds was one minute. These rules were adopted all over the world, and the rules governing boxing today in the United States are based on them.

Until the 20th century, there was very little boxing in countries outside of England and the United States—but it has since spread all over the world.

DID BASEBALL REALLY ORIGINATE IN AMERICA?

For us even to consider this question must seem shocking to many people. After all, isn't baseball our "national game?"

And in fact, almost every book on the subject gives Abner Doubleday the credit for inventing baseball. He is said to have laid out the first baseball diamond in Cooperstown, New York, in 1839, and set up the rules which baseball still follows today.

In 1907, a commission was appointed to investigate the origins of baseball and to settle the controversy about it once and for all. This commission published its report in 1908 in which it said that baseball was a distinctly American game, that Doubleday had invented it, and that baseball had nothing to do with any foreign games.

Some people, however, claim that this commission didn't really try to investigate the origin of baseball; its purpose was to prove that it was an American game. A great deal of information has since been published to support this point of view.

Let's consider some of it. The name "baseball" itself was used to designate a popular English game that goes back to the 18th century! A book printed in England in 1744 and reprinted in the United States in 1762 and 1787 describes a game of "baseball" which shows a player at the plate with a bat, a catcher behind him, a pitcher, and two bases. In fact, there are many references in books published before 1830 regarding baseball and even baseball clubs!

But the chief document that ties up the first forms of our baseball with an English game called "rounders" is a book published in London in 1828. It describes a game with a diamond, four bases, in which there are fouls, strike-outs, home runs, and so on. The runner, however, was put out by being hit by the ball. And it is claimed that Doubleday taught the game of baseball also with a runner being put out by being hit by the ball!

So perhaps baseball wasn't really invented in America, after all! There's no question, however, that we developed it into the game it is today.

WHAT WAS THE FIRST MOTION PICTURE?

A curious thing about the development of motion pictures is that the first people who made it possible weren't interested in movies at all! The first inventions were by men who wanted to study the movements of animals.

Even Thomas Edison, who perfected a device called "a kinetoscope" in 1893, thought of it only as a curiosity. But there were many other people who saw great possibilities for entertainment in these inventions and they began to make movies.

At first they were only scenes of something that moved. There were waves on the beach, horses running, children swinging, and trains arriving at stations. The first film which really told a story was produced in the Edison Laboratories in 1903. It was *The Great Train Robbery,* and it caused a nation-wide sensation.

The first permanent motion-picture theatre in the United States opened in November, 1905, in Pittsburgh, Pennsylvania. This theatre was luxuriously decorated and the owners called it "the Nickelodeon." Soon, all over the country, other Nickelodeons were opened.

D. W. Griffith, a former actor, was among the most famous of the early directors and producers. He was the first man to move a camera during a scene and he perfected modern editing technique. He invented the closeup and many other parts of motion picture art. In 1914, he produced *The Birth of a Nation,* one of the most spectacular pictures of all time. This picture about the Civil War cost more than $750,000 and was the most expensive film made up to that time.

Hollywood became the movie capital of the world after Cecil B. de Mille and Jesse Lasky began making a movie there called *The Squaw Man.* Soon other companies came to Hollywood and modern movies were on their way.

WHO INVENTED TELEVISION?

Television, as you know, is a rather complicated process. Whenever such a process is developed, you can be sure a great many people had a hand in it and it goes far back for its beginnings. So television was not "invented" by one man alone.

The chain of events leading to television began in 1817, when a Swedish chemist named Jons Berzelius discovered the chemical element "selenium."

Later it was found that the amount of electrical current selenium would carry depended on the amount of light which struck it. This property is called "photoelectricity."

In 1875, this discovery led a United States inventor, G. R. Carey, to make the first crude television system, using photoelectric cells. As a scene or object was focused through a lens onto a bank of photoelectric cells, each cell would control the amount of electricity it would pass on to a light bulb. Crude outlines of the object that was projected on the photoelectric cells would then show in the lights on the bank of bulbs.

The next step was the invention of "the scanning disk" in 1884 by Paul Nipkow. It was a disk with holes in it which revolved in front of the photoelectric cells, and another disk which revolved in front of the person watching. But the principle was the same as Carey's.

In 1923 came the first practical transmission of pictures over wires, and this was accomplished by Baird in England and Jenkins in the United States. Then came great improvements in the development of television cameras. Vladimir Zworykin and Philo Farnsworth each developed a type of camera, one known as "the inconoscope" and the other as "the image dissector."

By 1945, both of these camera pickup tubes had been replaced by "the image orthicon." And today, modern television sets use a picture tube known as "a kinescope." In this tube is an electric gun which scans the screen in exactly the way the beam does in the camera tube to enable us to see the picture.

Of course, this doesn't explain in any detail exactly how television works, but it gives you an idea of how many different developments and ideas had to be perfected by different people to make modern television possible.

CHAPTER 3
THE
HUMAN BODY

HOW DO WE GROW?

All living things grow. They grow in structure (shape, size, and how they are made), and in function (what they can do).

The most important forces that cause growth lie inside a living thing from its beginning. These forces are called its heridity. Animals, including human beings, have stages of growth. These are: embryo and fetus (not yet born), infant, child, youth, mature adult, and old age.

Some creatures have hardly any infancy. Some birds can fly as soon as they hatch. The guinea pig can take care of itself three days after birth. The human being is not an adult until he is about 20 years old.

At birth an infant already has all the nerve cells he will ever have—the cells in his brain, in his spinal cord, and those that reach out into every part of his body. The growth of the connections between these nerve cells will enable him to control his movements, to learn, and to behave like the people in his society.

So all human beings are much alike in their growth. But there are important differences. Boys and girls all follow the same general pathway of growth, but each one follows it in his own particular way and at his own speed.

People's bodies grow faster in the early weeks of life than at any other time. Even before the end of the first year, they are growing less rapidly. Through the whole period of childhood, they grow at a moderate rate. Then growth starts to speed up again.

For girls, this usually begins between ages 11 and 13, and for boys, between 12 and 14. For a while, they grow faster until they reach a top speed. Then they slow down again and grow more slowly until growth in height stops altogether. They have reached full size.

Growth in height and growth in weight often takes turns in a person. First he grows upward for a while, then sideways. For many people, there is a "chubby" period that happens somewhere around 11 or 12 years. But then their height begins to catch up in the next years and the chubbiness is gone.

WHY DO WE STOP GROWING?

The average baby is about one foot, eight inches long at birth. In the next 20 years, man triples the length of the body he was born with and reaches an average height of about five feet, eight inches.

Why doesn't he just keep on growing and growing? What makes the body stop getting bigger? In the body, there is a system of glands called the endocrine glands which controls our growth.

The endocrine glands are: the thyroid in the neck, the pituitary attached to the brain, the thymus which is in the chest, and the sex glands. The pituitary gland is the one that stimulates our bones to grow. If this gland works too much, our arms and legs grow too long and our hands and feet become too big. If the gland doesn't work hard enough, we might end up as midgets.

A child is born with a large thymus gland and it continues to get bigger during childhood. When a child reaches the age of 13 or 14, the thymus gland begins to shrink. The thymus gland and the sex glands may have a certain relationship. As long as the thymus gland is working, the sex glands are small. As the sex glands develop, the thymus gland stops working. This is why, when a person has become sexually mature at about the age of 22, he stops growing!

Sometimes the sex glands develop too soon and slow up the thymus gland too early. This often makes a person below average in height. Since our legs grow later and grow more than other parts of the body, this early development makes the legs short. That's why people who develop too early are often thickset. Napoleon was an example of this kind of person.

If the sex glands develop too late, the thymus continues working and the person becomes taller than the average. Actually, we continue growing slightly even after the age of 25, and we reach our maximum height at about the age of 35 or 40. After that, we shrink about half an inch every 10 years! The reason for this is the drying-up of the cartilages in our joints and in the spinal column as we get older.

WHAT MAKES US HUNGRY?

When we need food, our body begins to crave for it. But how do we know that we are feeling "hunger"? How does our mind get the message and make us feel "hungry"?

Hunger has nothing to do with an empty stomach, as most people believe. A baby is born with an empty stomach, yet it doesn't feel hungry for several days. People who are sick or feverish often have empty stomachs without feeling hungry.

Hunger begins when certain nutritive materials are missing in the blood. When the blood vessels lack these materials, a message is sent to a part of the brain that is called the "hunger center." This hunger center works like a brake on the stomach and the intestine. As long as the blood has sufficient food, the hunger center slows up the action of the stomach and the intestine. When the food is missing from the blood, the hunger center makes the stomach and intestine more active. That's why a hungry person often hears his stomach "rumbling."

When we are hungry, our body doesn't crave any special kind of food, it just wants nourishment. But our appetite sees to it that we don't satisfy our hunger with just one food, which would be unhealthy. For instance, it would be hard for us to take in a certain amount of nourishment all in the form of potatoes. But if we eat soup until we've had enough, then meat and vegetables until we've had enough, then dessert until we've had enough, we can take in the same quantity of food and enjoy it!

How long can we live without food? That depends on the individual. A very calm person can live longer without food than an excitable one because the protein stored up in his body is used up more slowly.

HOW DO WE DIGEST FOOD?

Taking food into our bodies is not enough to keep us alive and growing. The food must be changed so that it can be used by the body, and this process is called "digestion."

Digestion starts when food is put in the mouth, chewed, and swallowed, and it continues in the alimentary canal, which is a long, partly coiled tube going through the body. All parts of the alimentary canal are joined together, but they are different in the way they work. The mouth opens into a wide "pharynx" in the throat, which is a passage used for both food and air. The "esophagus" passes through the chest and connects the pharynx and stomach. The stomach leads into the coiled "small intestine." The last part of the alimentary canal is the "colon" or "large intestine."

Here is a quick picture of what happens to food during digestion. In the mouth, the saliva helps to break down starches (such as in corn or potatoes). When food has been moistened and crushed in the mouth, it goes down through the pharynx and along the esophagus, and finally enters the stomach.

It is in the stomach that most of the process of digestion takes place. Here, juices from the stomach wall are mixed with the food. Hydrochloric acid is one of these juices. Pepsin, another secretion, helps to break down proteins into simpler forms to aid digestion. The starches continue to break down until the material in the stomach becomes too acid. Then digestion of starches almost stops.

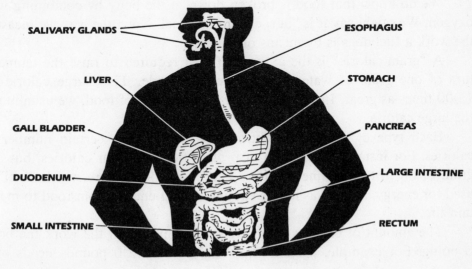

SALIVARY GLANDS

ESOPHAGUS

LIVER

STOMACH

GALL BLADDER

PANCREAS

DUODENUM

LARGE INTESTINE

SMALL INTESTINE

RECTUM

Food stays in the stomach until it is liquid. The materials in the stomach are churned about to mix digestive juices well throughout the foods. When the food is liquid it is called "chyme." The chyme moves out from the stomach into the small intestine through a valve at the lower end of the stomach, the "pylorus."

The small intestine is a tube from 22 to 25 feet long, which lies in coils. In the first part of the small intestine, the "duodenum," digestion continues. Juices from the pancreas and liver help break down the foods. The breakdown of proteins is finished here, fats are split into finer parts, and starch digestion is completed here. Digested food is absorbed here into the blood and lymph. In the large intestine, water is absorbed and the contents become more solid, so they can leave the body as waste material.

WHAT IS A CALORIE?

Nowadays, it seems, everybody is "watching their calories." There are even restaurants which print the number of calories each dish contains right on the menu! To understand what a calorie is and the part it plays in the body, let's start with the subject of nutrition in general.

Today, science is still not able to explain exactly how a cell transforms food into energy. We just know it happens. And we also can't explain why the cell in the body needs certain foods, and not others, in order to function properly.

We do know that food is broken down in the body by combining with oxygen. We might say it is "burned" up like fuel. Now, the way we measure the work a fuel does is by means of calories.

A "gram calorie" is the amount of heat required to raise the temperature of one gram of water one degree centigrade. The "large calorie" is 1,000 times as great. In measuring the energy value of food, we usually use the large calorie.

Each type of food, as it "burns up," furnishes a certain number of calories. For instance, one gram of protein furnishes four calories, but one gram of fat furnishes nine calories. The body doesn't care which "fuel" is used for energy, as long as it gets enough of that energy from food to maintain life.

The amount of calories the body needs depends on the work the body is doing. For example, a man who weighs about 150 pounds needs only

1,680 calories per day if he is in a state of absolute rest. If he does moderate work such as desk work, this jumps to 3,360 calories per day. And if he does heavy work, he may need as much as 6,720 calories a day to keep the body functioning properly.

Children need more calories than adults, since older people can't burn up the fuel as quickly. Interestingly enough, we use up more calories in winter than in summer. The normal fuels of the body are carbohydrates, starch, and sugar. Suppose, however, we take in more fuels than we need? The body uses up what it needs and stores some of it away for future use. The body can store away about one-third of the amount it needs each day. The rest becomes fat! And that's why we "watch our calories."

WHY DO WE PERSPIRE?

The body could be considered a permanent furnace. The food we take in is "fuel," which the body "burns up." In this process, about 2,500 calories are being used every day in the body.

Now this is quite a bit of heat. It's enough heat to bring 25 quarts of water to the boiling point! What happens to all this heat in the body? If there were no temperature controls in the body, we could certainly think of ourselves as "hot stuff." But we all know that the heat of the body doesn't go up (unless we're sick). We know that our body heat remains at an average temperature of 98.6 degrees Fahrenheit.

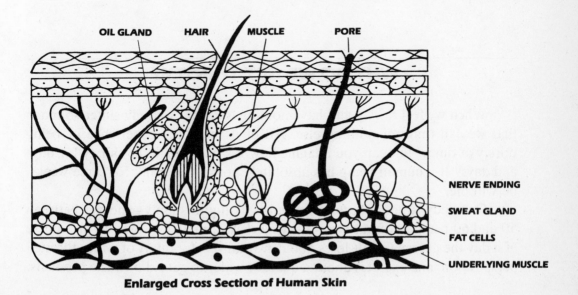

OIL GLAND   HAIR   MUSCLE   PORE

NERVE ENDING

SWEAT GLAND

FAT CELLS

UNDERLYING MUSCLE

Enlarged Cross Section of Human Skin

Perspiration is one of the ways we keep our body "furnace" at a nice normal temperature. Actually, our body temperature is controlled by a center in the brain known as the temperature center. It consists of three parts: a control center, a heating center, and a cooling center.

Suppose the temperature of the blood drops for some reason. The heating center goes to work and certain things begin to happen. Special glands give out more chemical substances to burn, the muscles and the liver use up more "fuel," and soon our internal temperature rises.

Now suppose the temperature of the blood rises for some reason. The cooling center goes to work. The process of oxidation, or burning up of fuel, is slowed up. And another important thing happens. The vessels in the skin are dilated, or opened, so that the extra heat can radiate away, and also to help our perspiration to evaporate.

When a liquid evaporates, it takes away heat. For example, we feel cold after a bath because the water which remains in contact with our warm skin is evaporating rapidly and cooling us off. So perspiration is part of the process of cooling the body.

Perspiration is like a shower which washes the body from within. The fluid flows out through millions of tiny openings in the skin in the form of miscroscopic drops. And these tiny drops can evaporate quickly and cool the body quickly when necessary.

On humid days, we suffer because the water on our skin can't evaporate easily. So we use fans to carry away the moist air and to help the evaporation of our perspiration.

WHY DO WE GET THIRSTY?

When we feel thirsty and have nothing to drink, we may suffer so much that we can think of nothing else. All of us have the experience of being thirsty at times—but can you imagine how it would feel to be thirsty for days and days? If a human being has absolutely nothing to drink for three weeks, he will die.

Our body simply needs to replenish its liquid supply—and yet between 50 and 60 per cent of our weight is water! As a matter of fact, in the course of a day the average adult loses about two-thirds of a quart of water through perspiration, and excretes about a quart of water to get rid of waste products.

On the other hand, whether we drink or not, we also take in water. When the body digests food, it obtains almost a third of a quart of liquid from this food per day. But this process of losing water and gaining it isn't enough to keep the balance of water our body needs. Thirst is the signal our body gives us that it needs more water.

Dryness in the mouth or throat is not what causes thirst, as many people believe. That dryness may be caused by many things such as nervousness, exercise, or just a slowing-up of the flow of saliva. It is possible to make the saliva flow again (for example, with a little lemon juice), but this will not take care of our thirst.

In fact, your saliva can be flowing freely, your stomach and blood stream and bladder may be full of water—and you can still be thirsty! For example, people who drink whiskey at a bar may have taken several drinks and still feel thirsty—if they happen to have munched on salty peanuts or pretzels between drinks!

The reason for this is that thirst is caused by a change in the salt content of our blood. There is a certain normal amount of salt and water in our blood. When this changes by having more salt in relation to water in our blood, thirst results.

In our brain, there is a "thirst center." It responds to the amount of salt in our blood. When there is a change, it sends messages to the back of the throat. From there, messages go back to the brain, and it is this combination of feelings that makes us say we're thirsty.

WHY DO WE GET TIRED?

Fatigue can actually be considered a kind of poisoning! When a muscle in the body works, it produces lactic acid. If we remove the lactic acid from a tired muscle, it's able to start working again at once!

In the course of a day, we "poison ourselves" with lactic acid. There are other substances the body produces in the course of muscular activity, which are known as "fatigue toxins." The blood carries these through the body, so that not only the muscle itself feels tired, but the entire body, especially the brain.

Scientists have made an interesting experiment about fatigue. If a dog is made to work until it is exhausted and falls asleep, and its blood is then transfused into the body of another dog, the second dog will instantly become "tired" and fall asleep! If the blood of a wide-awake dog is transfused into a tired, sleeping dog, the latter will wake up at once, no longer tired!

But fatigue is not just a chemical process; it is also a biological process. We can't just "remove" fatigue; we must allow the cells of the body to rest. Damages must be repaired, nerve cells of the brain must be "recharged," the joints of the body must replace used-up lubricants. Sleep will always be necessary as a way of restoring the body's energy after fatigue.

However, there is an interesting thing to remember about the process of resting. For example, a person who has been working hard at his desk for hours may not want to lie down at all when he's tired. He'd rather take a walk! Or when children come home from school they want to run out to play . . . not to lie down and rest.

The reason is that if only a certain part of the body is tired—say, the brain, the eyes, the hands, or the legs—the best way to make that part feel fresh again is to make other parts of the body active! We can actually rest by means of activity. Activity increases the respiration, the blood circulates faster, the glands are more active, and the waste products are eliminated from the tired part of the body. But if you are totally exhausted, the best thing to do is to go to sleep!

WHAT CAUSES OUR DREAMS?

Let us begin by saying what does not cause our dreams. Our dreams do not come from "another world." They are not messages from some outside source. They are not a look into the future, nor do they prophesy anything.

All our dreams have something to do with our emotions, fears, longings, wishes, needs, memories. But something on the "outside" may influence what we dream. If a person is hungry, or tired, or cold, his dreams may include this feeling. If the covers have slipped off your bed, you may dream you are on an iceberg. The material for the dream you have tonight is likely to come from the experiences you will have today.

So the "content" of your dream comes from something that affects you while you are sleeping (you are cold, a noise, a discomfort, etc.) and it may also use your past experiences and the urges and interests you have now. This is why very young children are likely to dream of wizards and fairies, older children of school exams, hungry people of food, homesick soldiers of their families, and prisoners of freedom.

To show you how what is happening while you are asleep and your wishes or needs can all be combined in a dream, here is the story of an experiment. A man was asleep and the back of his hand was rubbed with a piece of absorbent cotton. He dreamed that he was in a hospital and his sweetheart was visiting him, sitting on the bed and stroking his hand!

There are people called psychoanalysts who have made a special study of why we dream what we dream and what those dreams mean. Their interpretation of dreams is not accepted by everyone, but it offers an interesting approach to the problem. They believe that dreams are expressions of wishes that didn't come true, of frustrated yearnings. In other words, a dream is a way of having your wish fulfilled.

During sleep, according to this theory, our inhibitions are also asleep. We can express or feel what we really want to. So we do this in a dream and thus provide an outlet for our wishes, and they may be wishes we didn't even know we had!

HOW DOES OUR BLOOD CIRCULATE?

In very simple terms, the blood circulates because the heart "pumps" it and the veins and arteries act as "pipes" to carry it. The blood circulates to carry oxygen from the lungs and food materials from the organs of digestion to the rest of the body, and to remove waste products from the tissues.

The "pipes" are two systems of hollow tubes, one large and one small. Both are connected to the heart, the "pump," but do not connect with each other. The smaller system of blood vessels goes from the heart to the lungs and back. The larger goes from the heart to the various parts of the body. These tubes are called "arteries," "veins," and "capillaries." Arteries move blood away from the heart; the veins carry blood back to the heart. The capillaries are tiny vessels for carrying blood from arteries to veins.

Now a word about the "pump"—the heart. It is like a double two-story house, each with a room upstairs, called the right and left "auricles." The downstairs rooms are the right and left "ventricles."

If we were to trace a drop of blood as it circulated through the entire body, this is the course it would follow. The blood with oxygen from the lungs goes to the left auricle (upstairs room), then to the left ventricle

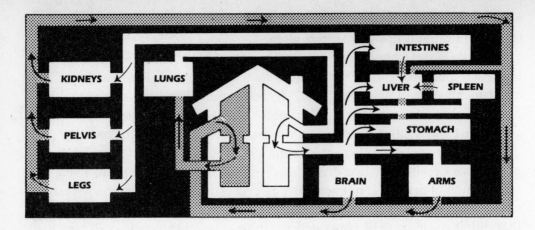

(downstairs room), and then to the "aorta." This is the great artery, and it and its branches carry the blood to all parts of the body.

Through the capillaries it goes from the smallest arteries into the smallest veins. It flows through the veins which become larger. Finally, it reaches the right auricle of the heart. Then into the right ventricle, and from there into arteries which carry it into the lungs. Here it gives up carbon dioxide and some water and takes up oxygen. Now it's ready to come back to the left auricle of the heart and start off on its journey again!

The heart squeezes and relaxes about 100,000 times each day and pumps about 3,600 gallons of blood in 24 hours in an adult male!

WHAT IS SKIN?

When we think of the human body, it is easy for us to think of the heart, or the liver, or the brain as "organs." They have certain jobs to do and they do them. But did you know that the skin is an organ, too?

Where other organs take up as little space as possible, the skin is spread out as thinly as possible to form a thin coat. In fact, this coat covers an area of 3,100 square inches. The number of complicated structures that appear in each one of these square inches is fantastic, ranging from sweat glands to nerves.

The skin consists of two layers of tissue. One is a thicker deep layer called the "corium," and on top of it is the delicate tissue called the "epidermis." These are joined together in a remarkable way. The bottom layer has "pegs" that project into the upper layer, and this is moulded over them to bind them closely together. Because these "pegs" are arranged in ridges, they form a kind of pattern which we can see in certain places on our skin. In fact, your fingerprints are made by these ridges.

The top layer of your skin, the epidermis, doesn't contain any blood vessels. It actually consists of cells that have died and been changed into "horn." We might say that the human body is covered with horn shingles. This is very useful to us, because horn helps protect us. It is insensitive, so it protects us from pain. Water has no effect on it, and it is even a good electrical insulator.

The very bottom layers of the epidermis are very much alive, however. In fact, it is their job to produce new cells. The new cells are pushed upward by the mother cells. In time, they are separated from their source of food and die to become horn.

Billions of the upper dead horn cells are removed every day in the natural course of our activities. But luckily, just as many billions of new cells are manufactured every day. This is what keeps our skin always young.

There are 30 layers of horn cells in our skin. Every time a top layer is removed by washing or rubbing, a new one is ready underneath it. We can never use up all the layers, because a new layer is always pushing up from the bottom. In this way, we are able to remove stains and dirt from our skins and keep it clean.

WHY DO PEOPLE HAVE DIFFERENT-COLORED SKIN?

People with the whitest skin are found in northern Europe and are called Nordics. People with the blackest skin live in western Africa. People in Southeast Asia have a yellowish tan to their skin. The majority of men, however, are not white, black, or yellow, but represent hundreds of shades of light, swarthy, and brown men.

What is the reason for these differences of color in the skin of people? The explanation really lies in a whole series of chemical processes that take place in the body and the skin. In the tissues of the skin there are certain color bases called "chromogens," which are colorless in themselves. When certain ferments or enzymes act on these color bases, a definite skin color results.

Suppose an individual either does not have these color bases, or his enzymes don't work properly on these bases? Then the person is an "albino" with no pigmentation at all. This can happen to people anywhere in the world. There are albinos in Africa, "whiter" than any white man!

Human skin itself, without the presence of any coloring substance, is creamy white. But to this is added a tinge of yellow, which is due to the presence of a yellow pigment in the skin. Another color ingredient found in skin is black, which is due to the presence of tiny granules of a substance called "melanin." This substance is sepia in color, but when it appears in large masses it seems black.

Another tone is added to the skin by the red color of the blood circulating in the tiny vessels of the skin.

The color of an individual's skin depends on the proportions in which these four colors—white, yellow, black, and red—are combined. All the skin colors of the human race can be obtained by different combinations of these color ingredients which we all have.

Sunlight has the ability to create melanin, the black pigment, in the skin. So people living in tropical areas have more of this pigment and have darker skin. But when you spend a few days in the sun, the ultra-violet light of the sun creates more melanin in your skin, too, and this results in the "sun tan"!

WHAT ARE FRECKLES?

To understand what freckles are and how they appear, we have to understand what gives skin its color in the first place.

The most important pigment in deciding the color of the skin is melanin. You might say that the different skin color of various races depends entirely on the difference in the amount of melanin.

In lower forms of life, by the way, it is the melanin which enables certain fish and lizards to change their colors. In the human being, its most important function, apart from controlling the color, is to protect us against the harmful effects of too much exposure to sunshine.

Melanin is produced by a whole network of special cells that are scattered through the lower layer of the epidermis, which is the thin, outer part of our skin. These cells are called "melanocytes." Now we come to the question: What are freckles? Well, freckles are simply a bunching-up of these melanocytes in spots. That's why freckles have that brownish color, the color of the pigment melanin. Why do some people have freckles and others don't? The reason is heredity. Our parents decide whether we'll have freckles!

The color of freckles (really the color of the melanin in them) can vary from light tan to dark brown, depending on exposure to sun and heat. Sunshine not only can darken them, but can cause new melanin to form.

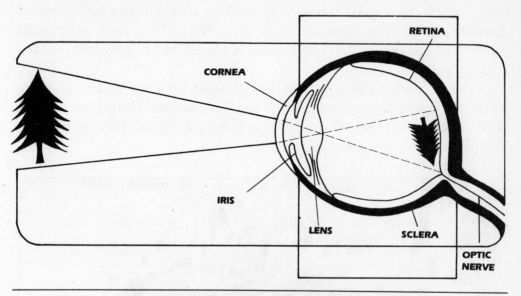

WHAT IS THE EYE MADE OF?

The human eye is like a camera. It has an adjustable opening to let in light (the pupil); a lens which focuses the light waves to form an image; and a sensitive film (the retina) on which the image is recorded.

Inside each human eye are about 130,000,000 light-sensitive cells. When light falls on one of these cells, it causes a quick chemical change within the cell. This change starts an impulse in a nerve fiber. This impulse is a message that travels through the optic nerve to the "seeing" part of the brain. The brain has learned what this message means so we know we are seeing.

The eye is shaped like a ball, with a slight bulge at the front. At the center of this bulge is a hole called the "pupil." It looks black because it opens into the dark inside of the eye. Light passes through the pupil to the lens. The lens focuses the light, forming a picture at the back of the eyeball. Here, instead of film as in a camera, is a screen of light-sensitive cells, called the "retina."

Around the pupil is the iris. It is a doughnut-shaped ring colored blue or green or brown. The iris can change in size like the diaphragm of a camera. In bright light, tiny muscles expand the iris, so that the opening of the pupil is smaller and less light passes into the eyeball. In dim light, the pupil is opened wider and more light is let in.

The entire eyeball is surrounded by a strong membrane called the "sclera." The whites of the eyes are part of the sclera. The sclera is transparent where the eyeball bulges in front. This part is called the "cornea." The space between the cornea and the iris is filled with a clear, salty liquid called the "aqueous humor." The space is shaped like a lens. It is, in fact, a liquid lens.

The eye's other lens is just behind the pupil. You can see what happens when this lens changes shape. When you look at near things, the lens becomes thicker in shape. When you look at distant objects, the lens becomes thinner.

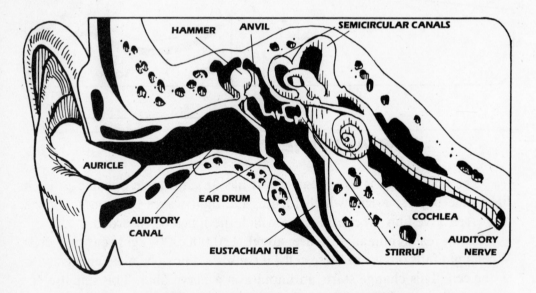

HOW DOES THE EAR WORK?

The ear is one of the most wonderful instruments in our body. Without our having to do any "tuning," it can pick up the tiny tick of a watch one moment and the roar of an explosion the next.

The ear, however, is not the only thing we need to be able to hear. The process of hearings begins with sound. Waves of air, which we call "sound waves," strike on the eardrum. We can neither see nor feel these waves, but the ear is so delicate that the slightest vibration is caught and passed on to the brain. Only when such waves reach the brain do we actually hear.

The ear is made up of three main parts: an outer ear, a middle ear, and an inner ear. Certain animals can move their outer ear forward to catch sounds more easily. But since we cannot move our outer ear, it doesn't really help us much in hearing.

When sound waves enter the outer ear, they travel down a canal. At the end of this canal is a thin skin, stretched tightly across a tube. This skin separates the outer from the middle ear, and it acts as a drum membrane. From the inner side of this drum a short tube, called the "Eustachian tube," leads to the throat. Enough air enters this tube by way of the throat to equalize the pressure caused by the vibrations on the other side of the drum membrane. Otherwise the membrane might be broken by loud sounds.

Directly behind the drum membrane in the middle ear are strung three curious little bones called the "hammer," the "anvil," and the "stirrup." They touch both the drum membrane and the inner ear. When sound waves strike the membrane, they start the three bones vibrating.

These bones, in turn, set up a series of vibrations in the fluid of the shell-shaped inner ear. In this shell, called the "cochlea," tiny cells transfer the sound to certain nerves. These nerves send them to the brain, which recognizes them, and that recognition we call "hearing."

In the inner ear there are also three semicircular canals which have nothing to do with hearing. They are also filled with a fluid, and they give us our sense of balance. If they are out of order, we become dizzy and cannot walk straight.

WHY ARE THERE DIFFERENT TYPES OF HAIR?

The kind of hair you have is a matter of inheritance. But the question is: Why are there so many different types of hair that might be inherited?

The general structure of the hair varies very little among human beings. But its form, its color, its general consistency, and the way a section of it looks under a microscope vary quite a bit. And because these differences occur in certain patterns, the hair is one of the best ways known to determine the race of a person. In other words, the hair you have inherited bears the stamp of your race.

There are three main classifications of hair by the way it's constructed. The first is short and crisp, the kind we call "woolly." A cross section of this hair shows it is elliptical or kidney-shaped. The color is almost always jet black, and it is the hair of all the black races with two exceptions.

The second type of hair is straight, lank, long, and coarse. A cross section of it look round. The color is almost without exception black. This is the hair of the Chinese, the Mongols, and the Indians of the Americas.

The third type of hair is wavy and curly, or smooth and silky. A section of it is oval in shape. This is the hair of Europeans. It is mainly fair with black, brown, red, or towy varieties.

There is also a fourth type, known as "frizzy," which is the hair of the Australian natives. Curly hair is generally hair that is quite flat in structure. The rounder the hair, the stiffer it is.

When it comes to color, some types have a range of colors, some do not. Wavy types of hair vary most in color. That's why, among Europeans, you can find the deepest black hair side by side with flaxen hair. But fair hair is more common in northern Europe and much rarer in the south. Among the races with straight hair, fair hair color is very rare. Races with frizzy hair have red hair almost as often as those with wavy hair. But red hair is related to the individual only—there are no races with red hair!

WHAT ARE FINGERNAILS MADE OF?

If every time you bit your nails you suffered pain, you'd probably never bite them. Or for that matter, if it hurt us to cut our nails there would be a great many people with very long nails!

But cutting, biting, filing our nails don't hurt us because the nails are made up of dead cells. The nails are special structures that grow from the skin. Most of the nail is made up of a substance called "keratin." This is a tough, dead form of protein, and a horn-like material.

At the base of the nail, and part of the way along its sides, the nail is embedded in the skin. The skin beneath the nail is just like any other skin except that it contains elastic fibers. These are connected to the nail to hold it firmly.

Most of the nail is quite thick, but at the point near the roots beneath the skin it is very thin. This part is white in appearance and has the shape of a semicircle or half-moon. It is called the "lunule." The fingernails grow about two inches a year.

Women, of course, have made the fingernails an object of beauty with nail colors and polishes. But to a great many people, the nails present all sorts of problems. One reason for many nail disorders is that the nails become injured. A burn or frostbite, for example, may injure nails so that they'll never grow again.

Nails that are very brittle, or hard, or that tend to split may be the result of many things: infections, a disturbance of the nutritional system, poor circulation of the blood, or even glandular disturbances.

Women who complain of peeling off of the nails at the tips may in many cases only have themselves to blame. They simply let their nails grow too long. Long nails are subject to shocks and this can result in damage to the nails.

HOW DO WE TALK?

The ability of man to speak is due a great deal to the way in which the larynx is made. This is a hollow organ, shaped something like a box. It is really an enlarged part of the windpipe. The walls of this "box" are made of cartilage and they are lined inside with mucous membrane.

At one place on each side, the mucous membrane becomes thicker and projects from the wall into the center of the box. These projections are the "vocal cords." Each cord is moved by many small muscles. When air goes from the lungs into the mouth, it passes between the two vocal cords and makes them vibrate. This produces a sound.

What kind of sound? It depends on the position and tension of these vocal cords. The muscle system that controls them is the most delicate muscle system in the entire body to make possible all the kinds of sounds we produce. Actually, the vocal cords can assume about 170 different positions!

When the vocal cords vibrate, the column of air that is in the respiratory passage is made to vibrate. What we really hear is the vibration of this column of air. If the vocal cords are not too tensed, long waves are produced and we hear deep tones. If the vocal cords are tensed, they vibrate rapidly, so short waves are produced and we hear high tones. When boys reach the age of about 14, the cords and the larynx become thicker and this makes the pitch of the voice lower. This change in pitch is called "change of voice."

So we see that the pitch of the sound we make is controlled by the tension of the vocal cords. Now how about the tone? This is determined by the resonating spaces, just as the tone of a violin is determined by the vibrations of the entire instrument. In speaking or singing, the resonating spaces involved include the windpipe, the lungs, the thorax, and even the spaces in our mouth and nose. The vibration of air in all of them helps decide the tone.

But that isn't all. Our abdomen, chest, diaphragm, tongue, palate, lips, teeth also get into the picture! All of them are involved in producing sounds and letters. So you see that the process of speaking is like playing on a very complicated and difficult musical instrument. It is only because we learned it early in childhood and practice it continuously that we are able to do it so well!

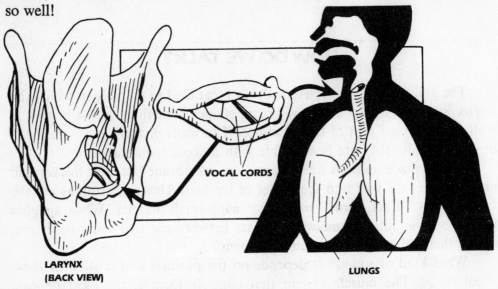

VOCAL CORDS

LARYNX
(BACK VIEW)

LUNGS

WHY ARE SOME PEOPLE LEFT-HANDED?

Many parents of left-handed children worry about this condition and wonder if they shouldn't try to correct it. The answer given by most authorities is: No! If there is a strong preference for the left hand, and the person is able to perform well with it, there should be no interference.

About four per cent of the population is left-handed. In the course of history, many of the greatest geniuses have been left-handed! Leonardo da Vinci and Michelangelo, the greatest sculptors of all times, were both left-handed.

Of course, we live in a "right-handed society"—that is, most of the things we use are made for right-handed people. Our doorknobs, locks, screwdrivers, automobiles, musical instruments—even the buttons on our clothes —are arranged for right-handed people. This may cause a certain amount of adjustment to be made by left-handed people, but most of them can manage quite well.

There is no single accepted explanation of what makes most people right-handed and a small minority left-handed. Here is one theory: The body is not "symmetrical," that is, it is not exactly the same on both sides. The right side of our face is a little different from the left. Our legs differ in strength. Our feet may differ a tiny bit in size. And this "asymmetry" goes through our whole body.

Now when we come to the brain, we discover that while it has a right half and a left half, these two halves don't function the same way. It is believed that the left half of the brain is "predominant" over the right half.

The nerves from the brain cross over at the level of the neck and go to the opposite side of the body. The right half of the brain supplies the left half of the body, and vice versa.

Now since the left half of the brain predominates, the right half of the body is more skilled, better able to do things. We read, write, speak, and work with the left half of the brain. And this, of course, makes most of us right-handed, too. But in the case of left-handed people, there is an "inversion." The right half of the brain is predominant, and such a person works best with the left side of his body!

WHAT CAUSES HICCOUGHS?

In England, there's an old superstition about how to get rid of hiccoughs. It goes like this: "To cure the hiccoughs, wet the forefinger of the right hand with spittle, and cross the front of the left shoe three times, saying the Lord's Prayer backwards."

You've probably heard of dozens of other "prescriptions" for getting rid of hiccoughs, most of them just about as effective as this old superstition! Hiccoughs really have nothing mysterious about them. They are the result of an action the body takes to protect itself. Let's see how this is so.

The body, as you know, has many reflexes. A reflex is a response on the part of the body to some sort of specific stimulation. This response is always the same, and seems to take place because certain nerve connections have been built up in our nervous system. We don't "decide" what action to take; the nerve connections spring into action without our control when there is a reflex action.

Now there are whole series of reflexes that have to do with getting solid and liquid food into our system and with getting rid of these or other foreign objects from air passages into which they sometimes go. For example, there are a whole series of reflexes connected with swallowing food. When food goes "the wrong way," the gagging and choking are reflex actions trying to expel the food.

Sneezing and coughing are actually normal reflexes in which a blast of air is used to help the body get rid of material it doesn't want. Vomiting is a very strong reflex action of this same type. And hiccoughing can be considered a sort of half-hearted and ineffective effort to vomit!

Hiccoughs can start because hot food has irritated some passage inside, or when gas in the stomach presses upward against the diaphragm. The diaphragm separates the chest from the stomach. The diaphragm tightens and pulls air into the lungs. But air can't get through and we feel a "bump" at the moment the air is stopped. So hiccoughs are a reflex action of the body trying to get food or gas out of the stomach, thereby irritating the diaphragm, which in turn affects the passage of air in and out of the lungs. We feel this as a "bump" and say we have the hiccoughs!

WHAT MAKES PEOPLE SNEEZE?

For some strange reason, the act of sneezing has long been considered more than just a physical action. All kinds of ideas and legends have grown up about sneezing, as if it had special significance.

Actually sneezing is the act of sending out air from the nose and mouth. It is a reflex act, and happens without our control. Sneezing occurs when the nerve-endings of the mucous membrane of the nose are irritated. It can also happen, curiously enough, when our optic nerve is stimulated by a bright light!

The irritation that causes sneezing may be due to a swelling of the mucous membrane of the nose, as happens when we have a cold; it may be due to foreign bodies that somehow get into the nose; or it may be due to an allergy. The act of sneezing is an attempt by the body to expel air to get rid of the irritating bodies.

From earliest times, however, people have wondered about sneezing, and it has universally been regarded as an omen of some kind. The Greeks, Romans, and Egyptians regarded the sneeze as a warning in times of danger, and as a way of foretelling the future. If you sneezed to the right, it was considered lucky; to the left, unlucky.

The reason we say "God bless you" after someone sneezes cannot be traced to any single origin, but seems to be connected with ancient beliefs. The Romans thought a person expelled evil spirits when he sneezed, so everyone present would say "Good luck to you" after a sneeze, hoping the effort to expel the spirits would succeed.

Primitive people believed that sneezing was a sign of approaching death. When anyone sneezed, therefore, people said "God help you!" because the person sneezing was in danger.

There is a legend that before the days of Jacob, a person died after sneezing. Jacob interceded with God, according to this tale, so that people could sneeze without dying—provided a benediction followed every sneeze!

During the sixth century there was a plague in Italy, and Pope Gregory the Great ordered that prayers be said against sneezing. It was at this time that the custom of saying "God bless you!" to persons who sneezed became established.

WHAT IS HAY FEVER?

If you don't suffer from hay fever, watching someone who does presents quite a mystery. Here you are living side by side, breathing the same air, and you go about feeling perfectly fit, while the other person sneezes constantly and suffers a great deal!

Hay fever is a form of allergy. It belongs to a group of maladies, including hives, asthma, and certain skin problems, that are caused by something called "protein sensitization."

Let us examine what this means. Protein, as we know, is found in foods. But it so happens that the pollens of plants are also protein. At a certain time of the year, many kinds of grasses, such as ragweed, send their pollens into the air in great amounts.

They reach human beings through the nose, mouth, and eyes. If the person whom they reach is not protein-sensitive, nothing happens. But when a person is abnormally sensitive to these proteins, they act upon certain

RAGWEED   GOLDENROD

muscles and tissues and cause those reactions that make them feel miserable.

A person may be sensitive to several different pollens, which is why the treatment of hay fever is a bit complicated. All the causes of the attack of hay fever have to be identified. Some patients are helped by injections of pollen or protein extracts which seem to build up an immunity. Other patients simply try to live in some other section of the country where the troublesome pollens don't exist.

WHAT CAUSES HEADACHES?

The answer to this question might be: anything and everything! A headache can start for any one of hundreds of reasons. You see, a headache is not a sickness or a disease. It is a symptom. It simply is a way of knowing that there is some disorder somewhere—in some part of the body or the nervous system.

Of course we know something about the "mechanism" of a headache, that is, what happens in the body or nervous system to produce the pain of a headache. The pain itself comes from certain structures in the skull. The large veins and others in the brain that drain the surface of the brain are sensitive to pain. It is not the brain substance itself but the coverings of the brain and the veins and arteries that are sensitive. When they "hurt," you have a headache. Also, when your sinuses, teeth, ears, and muscles hurt, the pain may spread to the brain area and produce a headache. If the muscles that are over the neck and near the head are contracted, this can also produce headaches.

When you listen to people talk about their headache problems, you hear them give personal reasons. But most of these are conditions that apply to many people. For example, some people get a headache when they're hungry, others say going without their "morning coffee" produces a headache, or it may be from a "hangover." What is really happening in all these cases is that the arteries in the skull are being dilated (or enlarged)—and this produces a headache in practically anybody. It's known as a "vascular headache."

Or suppose somebody suddenly had a vigorous jolt or twisted his head and began to complain of a headache. There's nothing special about such cases. What happened was that certain pain-sensitive structures in the brain were pulled or tightened and pain resulted. A person may be undergoing great emotional tension and this will cause muscles to contract or tighten over the back, lower part of the head, and neck. Result? A headache!

"Migraine" headaches are a special kind of headache and quite different from these. But as you can see, the symptom of disorder we call a "headache" has many, many causes!

WHAT IS A "COLD"?

Almost everybody knows the joke about the doctor who tells the patient who has a cold: "If you only had pneumonia, I could cure you." The cold is not only one of the most annoying afflictions man has to bear, but one of the most mysterious, as well.

More than 90 per cent of the people in the United States get a cold every year, and more than half of them get several colds during the year. You probably know the symptoms of a cold as well as your doctor does. There's a "running" nose, you sneeze a lot, you might have a sore or tickling throat, and sometimes a headache. Later on, a cough or fever may develop.

In an adult, a cold is seldom serious. But in children, the cold symptoms may actually be the early symptoms of more serious childhood diseases, such as measles or diptheria. That's why colds in children should have prompt medical attention.

A cold takes from one to three days to develop. There are three stages of the common cold. The first is the "dry" stage, which doesn't last long.

Your nose feels dry and swollen, your throat may have a tickle, and your eyes may water a bit. In the second stage, you get the "running" nose. And finally, that nose is really "running" and you may have fever and be coughing.

Now as to the great mystery. What is the common cold? What causes it? We can describe it as an acute inflammation of the upper respiratory tract—but that doesn't help much. Medical science simply doesn't know the specific cause of the common cold!

It is generally believed, however, that the infection is caused by a virus of some kind. But here's the strange thing: That virus is probably in your throat most of the time. It simply doesn't attack until your body resistance is lowered. There may also be other bacteria present and they don't attack either until your resistance is low. So it seems that the cold virus weakens the tissues so that other germs can infect them.

The best way to avoid a cold, therefore, is to keep your resistance high with a good diet, plenty of rest and sleep, proper dress, and avoiding contact with people who have colds.

WHY DO WE GET FEVER?

The first thing your doctor, or even your mother, will do when you don't feel well is take your temperature with a thermometer. They are trying to find out whether you have "fever."

Your body has an average temperature of 98.6 degrees Fahrenheit when it is healthy. Disease makes this temperature rise, and we call this higher temperature "fever." While every disease doesn't cause fever, so many of them do that fever is almost always a sign that your body is sick in some way.

Your doctor or nurse usually takes your temperature at least twice a day and puts it on a chart, showing how your fever goes up and down. This chart can often tell the doctor exactly which disease you have. A fever chart for pneumonia, for instance, goes up and down in a certain way. Other diseases have other patterns or "temperature curves" on the chart.

The strange thing is that we still don't know what fever really is. But we do know that fever actually helps us fight off sickness. Here's why: Fever makes the vital processes and organs in the body work faster. The body produces more hormones, enzymes, and blood cells. The hormones and enzymes, which are useful chemicals in our body, work harder. Our blood cells destroy harmful germs better. Our blood circulates faster, we breathe faster, and we thus get rid of wastes and poisons in our system better.

But the body can't afford to have a fever too long or too often. When you have a fever for 24 hours, you destroy protein that is stored in your body. And since protein is mighty necessary for life, fever is an "expensive" way to fight off disease!

WHAT IS CANCER?

As you probably know from the appeals being made for funds to fight cancer, and from all the research that is being done on this subject—cancer is a great menace to the health and life of mankind. We will only discuss cancer in general terms, so you can have an idea of what happens in a body that has cancer.

A cancer is a continuous growth in the body which doesn't follow the normal growth pattern. The cells forming the cancer spread through the body to parts which may be far from the spot where the cancer began. Unless it is removed or destroyed, the cancer can lead to the death of the person.

Cells in the body are growing all the time. As they wear out and disappear, their places are taken by new cells of exactly the same kind. But cancer cells look and act differently from normal body cells. They look like the young cell of the part of the body where they started—but different enough to be recognized as cancer when seen through a microscope.

When these cancer cells divide and increase in number, they don't change into the fully grown form and then stop reproducing. Instead, they remain young cells and continue to increase in number until they are harmful.

As the cancer cells grow, they do not remain in one spot, but separate and move in among the normal cells. They may become so numerous that the normal cells in this part of the body cannot continue to work or even remain alive. When the cancer gets into the blood, it is carried to distant parts of the body. There it may grow to form large masses which interfere with the activities of the normal cells.

Unless the growth and spread of the cancer is stopped, the patient will die. That's why it's important to have periodic examinations to detect and treat cancer before it has spread too far.

Cancers are not spread from man to man by contact. No drug has been found that cures completely and is useful for all kinds of cancer. One of medicine's greatest goals is to understand fully the nature and cause of cancer, and to find a way to prevent and cure it.

CHAPTER 4
HOW OTHER CREATURES LIVE

CAN ANIMALS UNDERSTAND EACH OTHER?

If we mean can animals communicate with each other, that is, pass on certain messages by signs and sounds, the answer is yes. If we mean can they talk to each other as we do, the answer is no.

Even among human beings, all communication is not by means of words. We have expressions to indicate anger, a shrug of the shoulder to indicate indifference, nodding and shaking the head, gestures with hands, and so on. Many animals make noises and signs to do the same thing.

When a mother hen makes a loud noise or crouches down, all her chicks understand this as a warning of danger. When a horse neighs or paws the ground, the other horses "get the message." Some animals can follow very slight signs or signals given by other animals. When a bird merely flies up to a branch to look around, the other birds don't move. But if a bird flies up in a certain way, they can tell it's about to fly off and they may follow.

Dogs communicate in many ways. They not only bark, but they howl, growl, snarl, and whine. They lift a paw, or bare their teeth. Other dogs can understand what these sounds and actions mean.

Animals communicate with each other not only with sounds and movements, but with smell. Most animals that live in herds depend on smell to keep together. And, of course, we know how dogs recognize each other by smell.

Apes are supposed to be among the most intelligent of animals, yet they really have no better "language" than other animals. They make many sounds and expressions of the face to communicate their feelings of anger or hunger or joy, but they have nothing like the words of human speech.

By the way, unlike human beings who have to learn how to talk, apes and other animals know their "language" by instinct. They will make the right kind of cries and sounds and expressions even if they have never seen another animal like themselves before.

Birds, however, learn their way of singing, at least in part. That's why a sparrow brought up among canaries will try to sing like one. It has been learning the wrong "language"!

DO ANIMALS LAUGH OR CRY?

If you have a pet, such as a cat or a dog, you may become so attached to it that in time you almost feel it's "human." That is, you begin to think it can express the way it feels in terms of human emotions, such as crying, or perhaps even laughing.

But this isn't really so. Crying and laughing are human ways of expressing emotions and no animals have this way. Of course, we know that animals can whimper and whine when they are hurt, but crying involves the production of tears with this emotion, and animals cannot do this.

This doesn't mean that animals don't have the tear fluid in their eyes. But it is used to irrigate the cornea of the eye. A creature must be a thinking and emotionally sensitive person to cry. Even children begin to cry only when they learn to think and feel. An infant yells, but he is not crying.

Crying is a substitute for speaking. When we cannot say what we feel, we cry. It is a reflex that happens despite ourselves and that helps us "get out" what we feel.

Laughter is also a human phenomenon. Some animals may give the impression that they laugh, but it is not at all like human laughter. The reason is that man always laughs at something, and this means that a certain mental process or emotion is involved. Animals are incapable of having such a mental process or emotion.

For example, when we laugh at a joke, or at a "funny" sight, our minds or our emotions make it seem laughable. In fact, there are many kinds of laughter and many reasons why we laugh. We may laugh at the ridiculous (a big, fat man with a tiny umbrella), or at the comic (a clown, for example), or at the humorous (a joke), and so on. We may even laugh in scorn.

Psychologists also believe that laughter is a social phenomenon. We laugh when we are part of a group that finds something amusing. Animals, of course, cannot resort to laughter for any of these reasons.

CAN ANIMALS TASTE?

Our sense of taste is a source of great pleasure to us. It makes the enjoyment of food possible. But we have a sense of taste not just to give us pleasure, but to protect us, too. It often prevents us from eating things that might harm us.

What is the process of tasting? It is the ability to perceive the impact of molecules. These moving molecules stimulate the taste nerves and we identify the message we receive as having a certain taste. Only substances that are in solution, where the atoms move about freely, can be tasted. A piece of glass, for example, has no taste. Everything that makes the molecules move about more intensifies the taste. That's why hot things have more taste than cold things.

The sensation of taste is first received by taste buds, which are really nerves constructed like buds. They have the special ability to pick up certain sensations which we call taste.

These taste buds are located, in man and the higher animals, on the tongue. The number of taste buds varies greatly, depending on the taste needs of the particular species of animal. Man, for example, is only a moderate taster. We have about 3,000 taste buds. A whale, which swallows whole schools of fish without even chewing, has few or no taste buds.

A pig, oddly enough, is more particular in its tastes than man, and has 5,500 taste buds. A cow has 35,000 taste buds, and an antelope has as many as 50,000 taste buds! So you see that not only can animals taste, but many of them are more sensitive tasters than man.

Animals that live in the sea often have taste buds all over their body. Fish, for example, taste with the whole surface of the body, right down to their tails! Flies and butterflies can actually taste with their feet. When the last joint of a butterfly's leg touches something sweet, its snout stretches out immediately so it can suck it up.

Snakes and lizards use their tongues for tasting, but not as we do. The tip of the tongue flickers out and picks up particles. It brings them to a special organ in the roof of the mouth which smells or tastes them!

CAN ANIMALS SEE IN COLOR?

The world is so bright with color everywhere we turn that it's hard to imagine that other creatures don't see it as we do. But how can we find out whether animals can see color when they can't tell us?

Scientists have made many experiments to get the answer. The bee has been the subject of hundreds of these tests, because we have been curious to know whether the bee tells flowers apart by their color. In one experiment, a bit of sirup was put in front of a blue card, and no sirup in front of a red card. After a while, the bees would come to the blue card, no matter where it was placed, and even if it had no sirup in front of it. This proved they could tell colors apart.

Two strange things were found out about the bee's ability to see in color. The first is that a bee cannot see red as a color. For a bee, it's only dark grey or black. The second is that bees can see ultraviolet as a color, while for human beings, it is just darkness!

Male birds have bright colors. Can female birds see those colors? In experiments done with hens, it was proven that they can see all the colors of the rainbow! But now comes a surprise. The animal that is probably closest of all to man as a friend, the dog, is color-blind! So far all experiments that have been made prove that the dog can't tell one color from another. Many times when we think the dog is responding to a color, he is really responding to some other clue or sign—smell, size, shape. Dog lovers should not be too disappointed by this because the dog's sense of smell is so great that it probably compensates for the inability to see in color. Cats, by the way, seem to be color-blind, too!

Monkeys and apes have a very good sense of color, but most other mammals are color-blind, including bulls!

The reason for color-blindness in mammals is connected with the fact that most of them hunt by night and don't depend on color, and also that they themselves are usually dull in color, so it isn't important in their lives.

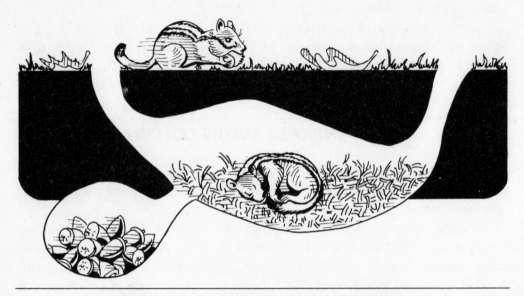

WHY DO ANIMALS HIBERNATE?

Let's look at the woodchuck as a typical hibernating animal. Unlike the squirrel, it doesn't store up a food supply for the winter. It depends on plant food, and when winter comes its food supply is gone. But the woodchuck has stored up a reserve supply of fat on its own body. So when it can no longer find food, it crawls deep into its burrow and goes to sleep. It sleeps through the cold winter and lives on the fat which it has stored up. The word "hibernate" comes from the Latin and means "winter sleep."

Many mammals, like the bear, do not really hibernate. They do sleep more in the winter than in summer, but it is not the deep sleep of hibernation. On warm and pleasant days in the winter, the bear, the squirrel, the chipmunk will wake up and come out into the open.

But the sleep of a true hibernator is almost like death and is quite unlike ordinary sleep. While an animal is hibernating, all its life activities nearly stop. The temperature of its body decreases until it is only a little warmer than the air of its den.

Because of this, the animals burn the food stored in their bodies very, very slowly. Since they burn less fuel, they need less oxygen, and as a result, their breathing is slower and their hearts beat only faintly. If the temperature in the den becomes very low, the hibernating animal wakes up, digs itself in a little deeper, and goes to sleep once more.

When spring comes, the animals are awakened by the change in temperature, moisture, and by hunger. They crawl out of their dens.

Did you know that many cold-blooded animals hibernate, also? Earthworms crawl down into the earth below the frost line; frogs bury themselves in the mud at the bottom of ponds; snakes crawl into cracks in the rocks or holes in the ground; and a few fish, such as the carp, bury themselves in the muddy bottom. Even some insects hibernate by hiding under rocks or logs!

WHY DOES A COW CHEW ITS CUD?

Many thousands of years ago, there were certain animals who couldn't protect themselves too well against their stronger, fiercer enemies. In order to survive, these animals developed a special way of eating. They would snatch some food hastily whenever they could, swallow it quickly without chewing, and run away to hide. Then when they were in their hiding place, sitting calmly, they would chew the food at their leisure!

Our "cud-chewing" animals are descended from these and are called "Ruminantia." It so happens that nearly all the mammals that are most useful to man are Ruminantia. These include cows, sheep, goats, camels, llamas, deer, and antelopes.

Here is what makes it possible for a ruminant like a cow to chew its cud. A ruminant has a complicated stomach with five compartments. These compartments are: the paunch or rumen, the honeycomb bag or reticulum, the manyplies or omasum, the true stomach or abomasum, and the intestine.

Each of these compartments of the stomach does something different to the food. When the food is swallowed, it is made into a coarse pellet and goes into the paunch, the largest of the five compartments. There it is moistened and softened and then passes into the honeycomb or reticulum.

Here it is made into balls, or "cuds" of a convenient size.

After a ruminant has eaten, it usually lies down or rests quietly somewhere. At this time it regurgitates the food from the reticulum back into the mouth. Now the ruminant chews the cud for the first time. After chewing, it swallows the food again and it goes into the manyplies, or third stomach. From here the food goes into the true stomach where the process of digestion takes place. Camels, by the way, differ from other ruminants in not having a third stomach.

Cows have no teeth in the upper jaw. Instead, the gum is in the form of a tough pad. This pad holds the grass down across the edges of the lower front teeth. When a cow grazes, it uses a sideways motion of the head to cut off the grass in this manner.

HOW LONG HAVE DOGS BEEN DOMESTICATED?

Hundreds of thousands of years ago, giant mammoths still roamed the earth and the world was covered with dense forests. Men lived in caves and dressed themselves in the skins of wild beasts. It was then that the dog first became man's friend.

At first the dog followed men on their hunting expeditions, to get whatever share he could of the kill. Then the instinct for companionship made him adopt man as his leader. Soon the men trained the dogs to help them in the hunt, to carry their burdens, and to guard their firesides. All this happened long before there was any recorded history. Actually, we can only guess at the story from finding the bones of primitive dogs with the bones of men in the caves of Stone Age.

Since the history of the dog goes back many hundreds of thousands of years, it is impossible to trace it clearly. Some scientists believe that dogs are the result of the mating of wolves and jackals. Other scientists say that some dogs are descended from wolves, other dogs from jackals, others from coyotes, and some from foxes. A widely held theory is that our modern dogs and the wolves are descended from a very remote common ancestor.

This theory helps to explain the differences in size and appearance of the various breeds of dogs and also explains their habits. When a dog turns around three times before he settles down to sleep, it may be because his remote ancestors had to beat down a nest among the forest leaves or jungle grasses. Other evidence of the wild ancestry of dogs is the build of their bodies, which is naturally adapted for speed and strength. This, together with their keen scent and quick hearing, were qualities they needed when they were wild hunters.

From the time there have been any permanent records of man's history, the dog has been mentioned. There are pictures of dogs on Egyptian tombs that are 5,000 years old. The Egyptians even considered the dog sacred, and when a dog died in an Egyptian home, the whole family went into mourning.

Though the dog has been loved and respected by most peoples of the world, there are some exceptions. The Hindus still consider the dog unclean and the Mohammedans despise dogs.

WHEN WERE CATS DOMESTICATED?

The cat has been around for a long, long time. Fossils of cats have been found which are millions of years old!

The domesticated cat we know today is the descendant of the wildcat, but just which wildcat we don't know, because it happened so long ago. Probably our varieties, or breeds, of domesticated cats all came from two or three of the small wildcats that existed in Europe, North Africa, and Asia thousands of years ago.

The best guess we have is that about 5,000 years ago these wildcats were domesticated for the first time. We know that 4,000 years ago the Egyptians had tame cats. In fact, the Egyptians worshipped the cat as a god. Their goddess Bast, or Pacht, was shown in pictures with a cat's head, and sacrifices were offered to cats.

The cat represented their chief god and goddess, Ra and Isis. When a house cat died, the Egyptian family and servants shaved their eyebrows and went into mourning. The death of a temple cat was mourned by the whole city. Many mummies of cats have been found, prepared in the same way as the mummies of kings and nobles. The penalty for killing a cat was death!

In Europe, however, there were probably no tame cats until after A.D 1000. In ancient times, the Europeans had quite a different attitude toward the cat than the Egyptians did. They thought of it as an evil spirit rather than a god. The devil was often pictured as a black cat, and witches were supposed to take the shape of cats.

The various breeds of domestic cats and individual cats vary from each other as much as the different breeds and individual dogs do. Probably the most easily recognized groups are the short-haired cats and the long-haired cats. The Angora and the Persian are the best-known long-haired cats.

WHY IS THE LION CALLED "KING OF BEASTS"?

Throughout the history of man, the lion has been considered the symbol of strength. We say "strong as a lion" or "lion-hearted." In courts throughout the world, the lion was used on shields and crests and banners to indicate power.

Probably this was not because anybody could prove that a lion could defeat all other animals in combat, but because lions strike such terror in man and in other beasts.

The ancient Egyptians believed the lion was sacred, and during the time when Christ was born, lions lived in many parts of Europe. By the year 500, however, they had all been killed. Today, the only places where lions are plentiful are in Africa and in one region of India.

Lions are members of the cat family. The average length of a grown-up lion is about nine feet and they weigh between 400 and 500 pounds. The males are larger than the females. People who hunt lions can always tell whether they are tracking a male or female by the size of the tracks. The male has larger front feet than the female.

The lion's voice is a roar or a growl. Unlike other cats, it doesn't purr, and rarely climbs trees. Unlike other cats, too, it takes readily to deep water. Lions feed on grazing animals, so they live in more or less open country and not in forests. And because they drink once a day, they always live near some supply of water.

Lions rest by day and do their hunting by night. Lions may live singly, or in pairs, or in groups of four to a dozen which are known as "prides." The main food supply of lions comes from zebras, gazelles, and antelopes. Sometimes a lion will attack a giraffe, but it won't attack an elephant, rhinoceros, or hippopotamus. When a lion isn't hungry, he pays no attention to other animals.

When hunting, a lion may lay hidden until an animal passes close by, or it may crawl and wiggle up to its victim and then make a sudden rush. When it makes that rush, it can go as fast as 40 miles an hour!

WHY DOES A MALE BIRD HAVE BRIGHTER COLORS THAN THE FEMALE?

To understand why this is so, we must first understand why birds have colors at all!

Many explanations have been given for the coloring of birds, but science still doesn't understand this subject fully. You see, the reason it's hard to explain is that some birds are brilliantly colored, others dully. Some birds stand out like bright banners; others are difficult to see.

All we can do is try to find a few rules that hold true for most birds. One rule is that birds with brighter colors spend most of their time in tree-tops, in the air, or on the water. Birds with duller colors live mostly on or near the ground.

Another rule—with many exceptions!—is that the upperparts of birds are darker in color than the underparts.

Facts like these make science believe that the reason birds have colors is for protection, so that they can't easily be seen by their enemies. This is called "protective coloration." A snipe's colors, for instance, blend perfectly with the grasses of marshes where it lives. A woodcock's colors look exactly like fallen leaves.

Now if the colors are meant to protect birds, which bird needs the most protection, the male or the female? The female, because she has to sit on the nest and hatch the eggs. So nature gives her duller colors to keep her better hidden from enemies!

Another reason for the brighter colors of the male bird is that they help attract the female during the breeding season. This is usually the time when the male bird's colors are brightest of all. Even among birds, you see, there can be love at first sight!

WHY DO BIRDS SING?

The song of birds is one of the loveliest sounds in nature. Sometimes when we are out in the country and we hear birds singing, it seems to us they are calling back and forth, that they are telling one another something.

The fact is that birds do communicate with one another, just as many other animals do. Of course, at times the sounds birds make are mere expressions of joy, just as we may make cries of "Oh!" and "Ah!" But for the most part, the sounds that birds make are attempts at communication.

A mother hen makes sounds that warn her chicks of danger and causes them to crouch down motionless. Then she gives another call which collects them together. When wild birds migrate at night, they cry out. These cries may keep the birds together and help lost ones return to the flock.

But the language of birds is different from language as we use it. We use words to express ideas, and these words have to be learned. Birds don't learn their language. It is an inborn instinct with them. In one experiment, for example, chicks were kept away from cocks and hens so they couldn't hear the sounds they made. Yet when they grew up they were able to make those sounds just as well as chicks that had grown up with cocks and hens!

This doesn't mean that birds can't learn how to sing. In fact, some birds can learn the songs of other birds. This is how our mockingbird gets its name. If a sparrow is brought up with canaries, it will make great efforts to sing like a canary. If a canary is brought up with a nightingale, it can give quite a good imitation of the nightingale's song. And we all know how a parrot can imitate the sounds it hears. So we must say that while birds are born with the instinct to sing, some learning takes place, too.

Did you know that birds have dialects? The song of the same kind of bird sounds different in different parts of the world. This shows that in addition to their instinct, birds do quite a bit of learning in their lifetime when it comes to singing.

WHAT KEEPS A DUCK AFLOAT?

When we use the word "duck," we are really referring to a very wide variety of birds. It ranges from the familiar barnyard type to the wild traveler in the skies. In fact, the duck family includes swans, geese, the mergansers or fishing ducks, the tree ducks, the dabbling ducks, the diving ducks, and the ruddy ducks.

Most of the wild ducks breed from the Canadian border states to the limit of trees in the Far North. It is only in the winter that they travel to the Central and Southern States. But they stay in the South for only a short time. As soon as the ice breaks up in the North, they head for home, the ponds, streams, marshes, lake shores, and seacoast where they like to live.

Ducks have no problem living in icy waters. The reason they are able to stay afloat is that their outer coat of closely packed feathers is actually waterproof. A gland near the duck's tail gives off an oil which spreads over the feathers. Underneath this coat, a layer of thick down protects them further. Even the webfeet of a duck are designed to protect them from the cold water. There are no nerves or blood in the webfeet, so they don't feel the cold.

The ducks' feet and legs are set far back on the body, which helps them greatly in swimming. It also gives them that peculiar waddle when they walk. A duck can move through the air pretty rapidly, too, and in short flights ducks have been known to go as fast as 70 miles an hour!

Most ducks build their nests on the ground near water. They line the nest with delicate plants and with down from the duck's own breasts. This warm down covers the eggs when the female is away from the nest. A duck lays about six to fourteen eggs, and only the female sits on the eggs.

Ducks molt, or shed their feathers, after the breeding season. Since their wing quills are gone at this time, ducks cannot fly during their molting period. To protect themselves from their enemies, they stay very quiet so as not to attract attention.

There are about 160 different types of species of ducks in the world, and they are found on every continent except Antarctica. In North America, we have about 40 species.

HOW DO FISH BREATHE?

Hundreds of thousands of years ago, long before man appeared on the earth, there were already fish swimming about in the oceans. At that time, fish were the most highly developed form of life in existence. In fact, fish were the first backboned animals to appear.

Since that time, fish have developed in a variety of ways, so that today only a very few even faintly resemble the first primitive fish of the oceans.

As a general rule, fish are long and tapering in shape. Man has copied this shape in his construction of ships and submarines because it's the best shape for cutting through water quickly.

Most fish use their tails as a power engine and guide themselves with tail and fins. Except for a kind of fish called "lungfish," all fish breathe by means of their gills. A fish takes in water through its mouth. The water flows over the gills and out through the opening behind the covers of the gills. This water contains oxygen which the fish thus obtains to purify its blood, just as human beings take oxygen out of the air to purify their blood.

When the water is contaminated in some way, fish will sometimes attempt to come to the top and breathe in air, but their gills are not suited for using the oxygen in the air.

The blood of fish is cold, but they have nervous systems like other animals and suffer pain. Their sense of touch is very keen, and they taste, as well as feel, with their skin.

Fish are able to smell, too. They have two small organs of smell, which are located in nostrils on the head. Fish have ears, but they are inside the head and are called "internal ears."

The reason fish are usually dark on top and light underneath is that this helps protect them from enemies. Seen from above, they look dark like the ocean or river bed. Seen from below, they seem light, like the light surface water. There are more than 20,000 different kinds of fish, so you can imagine in how many different ways they live!

HOW DO FLYING FISH FLY?

If there were fish which actually "flew" through the air the way birds do, they would obviously do it by flapping their "wings," or fins. There are no fish which fly that way.

But flying fish do manage to get about in the air and this is how they do it. The "wings" of the flying fish are the front fins, but greatly enlarged. When the fish in in "flight," it spreads out these fins and holds them at an angle to the body. In some cases, the fish also spread the rear fins.

The fish gets into the air by swimming rapidly through the water with part of its body breaking the surface. It goes along this way for some distance, gathering speed by moving its tail vigorously. Then it spreads the fins and holds them stiffly, and the speed of its motion lifts it into the air!

A flying fish may sail or glide for a distance of several hundred yards in this way before it drops back into the water. Sometimes it strikes the crests of the waves and moves its tail in order to pick up additional power while it is in flight. By the way, the flying fish doesn't just skim over the water. It can fly high enough to land on the decks of large ocean liners.

WHY DO SALMON GO UPSTREAM TO SPAWN?

There are many things that creatures do to produce and protect their young that seem quite miraculous to us. After all, isn't it rather amazing the way birds build nests, or the way certain animals will fight to save their young from enemies?

The instinct that takes the salmon on the long trip upstream must be there because this is the best way new salmon can be born and grow. Not all salmon go to the headquarters of a stream to spawn. Some stay quite close to lower stretches of rivers. The pink salmon is an example of this. It spawns only a few miles above salt water. But in contrast there is the king salmon. It may travel as much as 3,000 miles up a river from the sea!

When the salmon enter fresh water, they are in fine condition, healthy and strong and fat. But as soon as they reach fresh water, they stop feeding. Sometimes they wear themselves out trying to reach the exact place they want to go deposit their eggs.

Since many of the rivers they have to ascend have rapids and falls and jagged rocks, the salmon are often very thin and straggly looking by the time they have spawned. But whether they are worn-out or still in fair condition, the Pacific salmon die after spawning.

When the fish reach the spawning spot (which is usually the very same spot where they were hatched!), the female digs a sort of hole in the gravel or sand with her body, tail, and fins. The eggs are deposited in this "nest" and are fertilized by the male. Then the female covers the eggs.

Now their job is finished and the salmon seem to lose all interest in life. They drift downstream more or less with the current, and then they soon die. Then life begins for the newly hatched fish, which may be about 60 days later.

The young salmon remain in fresh water for a few months or a year, then descend the streams and enter salt water. And so the cycle begins all over again!

RATTLESNAKE

WHICH SNAKES ARE POISONOUS?

Man seems to have always had a fear and horror of snakes. Their appearance, the way they move about, and the fact that many people have died of snakebite, is responsible for this fear.

There are more than 2,000 species or kinds of snakes. They live on land, in the earth, in water, and in trees. And they can be found in practically all parts of the world except the polar regions and some islands.

The poisonous snakes possess poison fangs, which are hollow teeth, with an opening at the tip. These poison-conducting teeth, or fangs, are in the upper jaw and connect with poison glands in the head. A poison-snake cannot be made permanently harmless by the removal of its fangs, because new fangs will be grown.

Snakes with poison fangs usually inject the poison into their prey to kill it or make it unconscious before it is eaten.

There are about 120 species of non-poisonous snakes in the United States. Poisonous snakes of the United States consist of only four types. One is the coral snake, of the cobra family. It occurs only in the South.

The other three types belong to the pit viper family, of which the rattlesnake, the copperhead, and the water moccasin are members. There are about a dozen kinds of rattlesnakes. All rattlesnakes may be considered as a type, and are easily recognized by the rattle on the end of the tail.

Rattlesnakes are found in practically all the states. The copperhead is found in the Eastern States from Massachusetts to Florida. The water moccasin lives in the Southeast.

This leaves quite a number of non-poisonous snakes in the United States. These are not only harmless, but are useful in destroying vermin. Among them are the blacksnake, milk snake, king snake, garter snake, green snake, and hissing "adder."

DO RATTLESNAKES RATTLE BEFORE THEY STRIKE?

A rattlesnake is certainly something to be afraid of. And because people are afraid of it, they have developed an idea that makes it seem a little less dangerous—that a rattlesnake will warn you before it strikes by rattling its tail.

Unfortunately, this isn't completely true. When a rattlesnake does rattle, it's usually because it has become frightened. This makes it vibrate its tail rapidly which causes the rattles to strike together. But studies of the rattlesnake have shown that about 95 per cent of the time this snake gives no warning at all before it strikes!

By the way, this idea of rattlesnakes and other poisonous snakes "striking" rather than biting isn't quite true, either. The fact is poisonous snakes both strike and bite, but some snakes bite more than others.

A snake with long fangs, like the rattlesnake, has its long, hollow, movable fangs folded inward against the roof of the mouth when the mouth is closed. When the snake is about to strike, it opens its mouth, the fangs fall into biting position, and the snake lunges forward. As the fangs penetrate the skin, the snake bites.

This biting movement presses the poison glands so that the poison flows out, then goes through the hollow teeth and into the wound. Other snakes, such as the cobra, which has shorter fangs, hold on for a time when they bite, and chew. This chewing motion forces the poison into the wound.

As a matter of fact, the cobra is a much more dangerous snake than the rattlesnake. The cobra is more aggressive, more likely to attack. And while a rattlesnake has more poison, the venom of the cobra is more deadly. People have been known to die from the bite of a cobra in less than an hour!

WHAT IS THE LARGEST SNAKE IN THE WORLD?

There are more than 2,000 different kinds of snakes. Snakes are such fascinating and frightening creatures that people have developed all kinds of wrong ideas about them. One of these is that there are huge, terrifying snakes 60 and 70 feet long!

The truth is that snakes never grow to quite that length, though some are certainly big enough. The largest known snake is the anaconda, which lives in tropical South America. A specimen shot on the upper Orinoco River in eastern Colombia was 37½ feet in length. But in such an isolated region, there may be even larger anacondas that have not yet been discovered.

A regal python bearing the name "Colossus" was the longest snake ever kept in a zoo. It was probably more than 29 feet long when it died at the Highland Park Zoological Gardens on April 15, 1963. At a weighing about six years earlier, it weighed 320 pounds. Most regal pythons are found in southeastern Asia and in the Philippine Islands.

The Indian python, found in India and the Malay Peninsula, may grow to a length of from 22 to 25 feet. The Africa rock python is about the same length. The diamond python of Australia and New Guinea often grows to 20 or 21 feet.

Then we come to a snake that, for some reason, is believed by many people to be the world's largest. It's the boa constrictor, and the most it ever measures is about 16 feet. This nasty creature makes its home in Southern Mexico, and Central and South America.

The king cobra, another unpleasant member of the snake family, reaches a maximum length of about 18 feet. Now what about the United States? What are the largest snakes we're ever likely to run into here? The longest of these is the Eastern diamondback rattlesnake, and it only grows to a length of about seven feet. The black chicken snake, bull snake, gopher snake—all found in the United States—also grow only to maximum lengths of about eight feet.

The longest poisonous snake is the king cobra, and the heaviest poisonous snake is the Eastern diamondback rattlesnake.

WHY DOES A WHALE SPOUT?

Whales are not fish but mammals. They are warm-blooded creatures whose young are not hatched from an egg but are born live. And the baby whale is fed on its mother's milk like other little mammals.

But whales, like all water mammals, are descended from ancestors that lived on land. So they had to adapt themselves for life in the water. This means that over millions of years certain changes took place in their bodies so that they could live in the water.

Since whales have no gills but breathe through their lungs, one of the most important changes had to do with their breathing apparatus. Their nostrils used to be up in the forward part of the head. These have moved back to the tops of their heads. They now form one or two blow-holes which make it easier for them to breathe at the surface of the water.

Under water these nostrils are closed by little valves, and the air passages are shut off from the mouth so that they are in no danger of taking water into the lungs.

Whales usually rise to breathe every five or ten minutes, but they may remain under water for three-quarters of an hour! On reaching the surface, they first "blow," or exhale the used air from their lungs. As they do this, they make a loud noise which may be heard for some distance. What does this spout consist of? It is not water, but merely worn-out air, loaded with water vapor.

They blow several times until they have completely changed the air in their lungs, and then they dive deeply, or "sound." Some whales have been known to dive 2,000 feet deep! Sometimes big whales, in sounding, throw their tails up into the air or even jump completely out of the water!

FROG TOAD

WHAT'S THE DIFFERENCE BETWEEN FROGS AND TOADS?

Many people wonder if there is a different between frogs and toads. While there are certain differences, in most important things, they are very much alike. They both belong to that group of cold-blooded creatures that live both in water and on land.

Most frogs and toads resemble each other very closely, and it's often hard to tell them apart. Frogs, however, are smooth and slippery, long and graceful. Most toads are dry, warty, and squat. Also, most frogs have teeth while most toads have none.

Almost all Amphibia lay eggs, so in this, the frogs and toads are alike. The eggs of both frogs and toads look like specks of dust floating on top of the water in a jellylike substance. The eggs hatch into little tadpoles, which look more like fishes than frogs or toads.

The tadpoles breathe through gills and have a long swimming tail, but no legs. The eggs develop into this tadpole stage in from three to 25 days. In about three or four months, the tadpoles lose their gills and their tails and develop legs and lungs. But it still takes about a year for the tadpole to become a frog or toad. Frogs and toads often live to a good old age, sometimes even as long as 30 or 40 years!

A toad lays fewer eggs than a frog, which means anywhere from 4,000 to 12,000 eggs every year, while a female bullfrog may lay from 18,000 to 20,000 eggs in one season! There are certain kinds of toads in which the male plays an important part in hatching the eggs. One kind of male toad found in Europe, for example, wraps the long string of eggs about his feet and sits in a hole in the ground with them until they are ready to hatch. He then carries them back to the pond.

A weird-looking toad which lives in South America hatches out its eggs in holes in its back! These holes are covered with skin, and are filled with a liquid. The young remain in these holes while they pass through the tadpole stage.

Toads which live in temperate regions are usually brown and olive, while those in the tropics are often bright-colored. It is not harmful to handle toads.

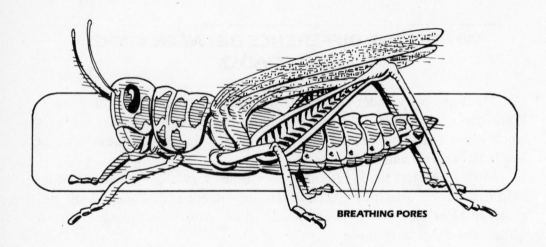

BREATHING PORES

HOW DO INSECTS BREATHE?

All living creatures must breathe in order to sustain life. Breathing is simply the taking-in of air in order to get oxygen, and the exhaling of a changed kind of air. The air we breathe out has had oxygen taken out of it and it has increased amounts of carbon dioxide and water.

The oxygen taken in is needed to "burn" certain food products so the body can use them. Waste products, including water and carbon dioxide, are eliminated by the body in part by being breathed out.

The simplest form of breathing is probably carried on by jellyfish and many worms. They have no breathing organs at all. Dissolved oxygen soaks through their skins from the water in which they live. Dissolved carbon dioxide soaks out. That's all there is to their "breathing."

An earthworm, which is more complicated, has a special fluid, the blood, to carry oxygen from the skin to the internal organs and bring carbon dioxide out. The frog sometimes breathes this way, too, using its skin as a breathing organ. But it has lungs for use when its body needs greater amounts of oxygen.

In insects, breathing takes place in a most unusual and interesting manner. If we examine an insect closely on the abdomen or belly, we see a large number of little openings or pores. Each of these pores is the entrance to a tube called a "trachea." This trachea works in the same way as man's breathing tube or windpipe! So an insect breathes the way we do, except that it may have hundreds of windpipes in its belly to take in air. In a creature as small as an insect, these tubes don't take up too much space. But can you imagine what would happen if man's breathing system were like the insect's? There would hardly be room for any other organs!

By the way, the rate of breathing (how often air is taken in) depends a great deal on the size of the creature. The larger it is, the slower the breathing rate. An elephant breathes about 10 times a minute, but a mouse breathes about 200 times a minute!

WHAT IS THE PURPOSE OF A FIREFLY'S LIGHT?

Is there anyone who hasn't been mystified by the light of the firefly? Children love to catch them and put them in bottles, or hold them in their hands while the little creatures flash on and off. Now, one thing that may surprise you is that scientists, too, have been mystified by the firefly's light. And they are still mystified—because there are many things about it they can't explain.

The light of the firefly is very much like other kinds of light—except that it is produced without heat. This kind of light is called "luminescence." In the firefly, luminescence is produced by a substance called "luciferin." This combines with oxygen to produce light.

But this reaction won't take place unless another substance, called "luciferase," is present. Luciferase acts as a catalyst; that is, it helps the chemical reaction take place but is not a part of it. To put it another way: fireflies have luciferin and luciferase in their bodies. The luciferase enables the luciferin to burn up and produce light.

Now, scientists can produce this same kind of light in the laboratory. But in order to do so, they must obtain the ingredients from the firefly! Chemists cannot produce them synthetically. It remains a secret of nature!

What is the purpose of this light in the firefly? Well, there are some explanations for it, of course. One is that perhaps this helps the fireflies find their mates. Another purpose might be to serve as a warning to night-feeding birds so that they will avoid the fireflies.

But scientists still feel that they don't really know why these lights are necessary to the firefly, since the above reasons don't seem important enough. They think the light may just be a byproduct of some other chemical process that goes on in the firefly's body. A light happens to be produced, but it's not a vital process. Well, whatever the reason for the light, I'm sure most of us are glad it's there—because of the pleasure of seeing these little insects as they move about at night.

HOW DO BEES MAKE HONEY?

The reason bees make honey is that it serves them as food. So the whole process of making honey is a way of storing up food for the bee colony.

The first thing a bee does is visit flowers and drink the nectar. Then it carries the nectar home in the honey sac. This is a baglike enlargement of the digestive tract just in front of the bee's stomach. There is a valve that separates this section from the stomach.

The first step in the making of the honey takes place while the nectar is in the bee's honey sac. The sugars found in the nectar undergo a chemical change. The next step is to remove a large part of the water from the nectar. This is done by evaporation, which takes place because of the heat of the hive, and by ventilation.

Honey stored in the honeycombs by honeybees has so much water removed from the original nectar that it will keep almost forever! The honey is put into the honeycombs to ripen, and to serve as the future food supply.

By the way, when bees cannot obtain nectar, they sometimes collect sweet liquids excreted by various bugs, or secretions from plants other than nectar.

Honey is removed from the hive by various methods. It may be squeezed from the comb by presses, or it may be sold in the combs cut from the hive. Most honey, however, is removed from the combs by a machine known as "a honey extractor." This uses centrifugal force to make the honey leave the comb.

Honeys vary greatly, depending on the flowers from which the nectar came and the environment where the hive is situated. Honey contains an amazing number of substances. The chief ingredients are two sugars known as levulose and dextrose. It also contains the following: small amounts of sucrose (cane sugar), maltose, dextrins, minerals, numerous enzymes, numerous vitamins in small amounts, and tiny amounts of proteins and acids.

Honeys differ in flavor and color, depending on the source of the nectar. In those areas where honey is produced, there are usually only a few plants that produce enough nectar to be a source of supply. Thus, in the Northeast United States, most honey comes from clover; in the West, it may come from alfalfa; in Europe, from heather; and so on.

HOW DOES A CATERPILLAR BECOME A BUTTERFLY?

Have you ever heard people say that a butterfly never eats? This happens to be true of some butterflies—and the reason lies in the story of how a caterpillar changes into a butterfly.

During her life, a female butterfly lays from 100 to several thousand eggs. She is very careful to lay these eggs near the kind of plant that will be useful to her offspring later. If there is only one such plant in a certain area—that's where she'll lay the eggs!

From these eggs hatch out tiny, wormlike grubs, called "caterpillar larvae." They begin at once to feed and grow, and as they grow they shed their skins several times. All the caterpillars do during this time is eat and eat—because the food they store away now may have to last them for the rest of their lives when they become butterflies! The food is stored as fat, and is used to build up wings, legs, sucking tubes, and so on, when the caterpillar becomes a butterfly.

At a certain time the caterpillar feels it's time for a change, so it spins a little button of silk, to which it clings. It hangs head down, sheds its caterpillar skin, and then appears as a pupa or chrysalis. The chrysalis clings to the button of silk by a sharp spine at the end of its body.

The pupa or chrysalis may sleep for some weeks or months. During this time, however, it is undergoing a change, so that when it comes out it is a full-grown insect. When it emerges from its chrysalid skin, it is a butterfly—but it doesn't do any flying at first. It sits still for hours to let its wings spread out and become dry and firm. It waves them back and forth slowly until it feels they are ready to use for flying—then off it goes on its first flight in search of nectar!

By the way, the life history of the moth is almost exactly the same as that of the butterfly. And did you know that there are many more different kinds of moths than there are butterflies? In North America, there are about 8,000 types of moths—and only about 700 kinds of butterflies.

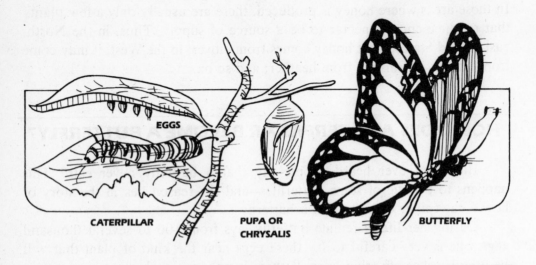

EGGS

CATERPILLAR

PUPA OR
CHRYSALIS

BUTTERFLY

HOW DO SILKWORMS MAKE SILK?

Thousands of years ago China had learned the secret of making silk cloth from the fine web spun by a certain caterpillar in making its cocoon. This secret was jealously guarded, and anyone who carried silkworms or their eggs out of China was punishable by death!

Today, of course, silkworms are raised in China, Japan, India, France, Spain, and Italy. The best silk is produced by the caterpillar of a small grayish-white moth which feeds on the leaves of the white mulberry.

In the early summer, each female moth lays 500 or more eggs. These eggs are carefully kept on strips of paper or cloth until the next spring when the mulberries open their leaves. Then the eggs are placed in incubators where they hatch out tiny black worms. The worms are placed in trays filled with finely chopped mulberry leaves and are fed constantly for about six weeks.

When the worms begin to move their heads slowly back and forth, they are ready to spin their cocoons. Little twigs are put in the trays to support them. The worms loop about themselves an almost invisible thread which they pour out through little holes in their jaws. The cocoon, which may contain as much as 500 to 1,200 yards of thread, is finished in about 72 hours.

Inside the cocoon is a shrunken chrysalis, which may develop into a moth in about 12 days. So the cocoons are exposed to heat to kill the chrysalises. The cocoons are placed in troughs of warm water to soften the silk gum which holds the filaments of the thread together.

Filaments from several cocoons are brought together into a single thread as they are unwound from the cocoons and wound on a reel. The threads from the reel are twisted into a skein of raw silk. This thread of 10 or 12 filaments is called a "single" thread of silk.

When you buy silk stockings marked "two-thread" or "three-thread," the markings are based on this thread of silk. Today, nylon has become so popular and so cheap that it has replaced silk in many uses. But silk will always be appreciated for its beauty, richness, and softness.

WHY AREN'T SPIDERS CAUGHT IN THEIR OWN WEBS?

"Won't you come into my parlor?" said the spider to the fly. The tricky spider is pretty clever, isn't he? He knows the fly will be caught and he'll be able to scamper along and have himself a nice meal!

But if the sticky web clings to the fly and traps him, why doesn't it cling to the spider? The answer to this will surprise you. It does! A spider can be caught just as easily in his own web as a fly is.

The reason this doesn't happen is that the spider is "at home" in his own web. He knows his way around. And when the web was spun originally, the spider made sure that there would be "safe" threads to use, threads he could touch without sticking to them.

There are many kinds of silk that a spider produces. The sticky kind is used in the web to catch prey. But there is also a non-sticky kind, and this is used to make the strong, supporting spokes of the web. The spider knows which is which, and he simply avoids the sticky ones! He can do this because he has a remarkable sense of touch.

WHAT DO ANTS EAT?

About the only place in the world where you won't find any ants is on the summits of the very highest mountains. So as you might imagine, there are thousands of different kinds of ants and how they live and what they eat depend on the species you are considering.

Let us see what are some of the unusual eating habits of certain ants. The harvester ant gathers seed from some grass common to the region and carries them into the nest. Here the seeds are sorted and stored away as the food supply.

Other ants are dairy farmers. They keep herds of plant lice, or "aphids," as they are called. They milk them by stroking their sides until the sweet liquid which they secrete oozes out. The ants relish this honeydew, or milk, so much that they take excellent care of their "cows."

Other ants grow fungi and live on nothing else. The fungus which they eat must have something to grow on. So the ants make a paste on which to raise the fungus, or mold.

Some ants are millers. One variety of ant has a special kind of worker with a huge head. The head holds powerful muscles to work its jaws and do the grinding. This worker ant is really the miller of the colony. It grinds up the grain that is brought in by the ordinary workers. After the harvest season is over, the millers are killed and their heads are bitten off. The reason this is done is the ants want no extra mouths to feed.

One kind of ant maintains living storehouses of food. As the worker ants bring in the nectar from the flowers, special ants in the colony take it and swallow it. During the winter, the other ants come to them and receive from their mouths enough nectar to feed themselves and the colony until the next season.

HOW DO EARTHWORMS EAT?

Earthworms have been called the most important animals in the world! Important, of course, from the point of view of human beings, because the activity of the earthworms prepares the soil for vegetation, upon which life depends.

Earthworms turn the soil over and break it up by eating it. In a single acre of garden, the worms in it will pass about 18 tons of soil through their

bodies in one year! Worms let air and water get to the plant roots. They turn under decayed plant and animal matter, and they even plant seeds. This is done when they drag leaves into their burrows and thus pull fine seeds from trees and plants below the surface, too.

The manure of earthworms, which is called "worm casts," contains lime which makes the soil rich. The importance of this can be seen when we consider what scientists discovered about the Nile Valley, one of the earth's most fertile regions. They estimated that about 120 tons of earthworm castings are deposited on each acre in the Nile Valley, and this is the real reason why this region has been fertile for hundreds of years!

There are so many earthworms in the soil of the United States that if all of them were weighed it would equal more than 10 times the weight of the human population!

The earthworm's body is made of two tubes, one inside another. The inner tube is the digestive system. When the worm wants to eat, it turns its throat inside out and pushes it forward to grip a piece of dirt. Then it draws the dirt back into the tube with its throat muscles. The dirt first goes into a storeroom called "the crop," and then into the gizzard. Grains of sand help the worm grind up the soil. Then it is digested, and the dirt is pushed from the body as "casting."

An earthworm has no eyes, but it has "sense-cells" on the outside of its body. This enables the worm to tell light from darkness and to feel the lightest touch. The earthworm breathes through its skin.

Earthworms live in fine, moist soil; they cannot live in sand. They come up only at night. During the winter they curl up into a ball and sleep. When you see a worm on the surface, it is because it is looking for a new home or a better feeding ground. Worms cannot live in the sunlight.

WHY DO MOTHS EAT WOOL?

There is a moth known as "the clothes moth," and most people blame it for making the moth holes in our clothes, furs, and rugs. But the moth doesn't do this damage at all!

The moth never eats. It lives only to produce its eggs and then dies. It is when the young moth is in the caterpillar stage that all the damage is done.

The eggs of the moth are laid on wool, furs, rugs, and so on. In about a week, the eggs hatch into caterpillars. What happens then depends on the kind of moth it is, since there are three different kinds of clothes moths in North America.

One is the case-making moth, which is most common in the Northern United States and Canada; the second is the webbing moth, which is usually found in the Southern States; and the third is the tapestry moth, which might appear in all sections.

The caterpillar of the case-making moth makes a little tubular case out of the wool it eats, and lines this case with silk. There it lives as a caterpillar. The caterpillar of the webbing moth always leaves a cobwebby trail of its silk and spins a silk cocoon. As the caterpillar of the tapestry moth eats into wool, it makes a series of tunnels which it lines with silk. When full-grown, it goes into one of these tunnels and stays there until it is ready to come out as a moth.

So you see that the problem of protecting clothes against moths is to make sure that no eggs are laid on the clothes. Before clothes are put away for the summer, they should be aired and brushed to make sure that there are no eggs or moths on them. It's a good idea to wrap them in heavy paper or in a tightly sealed cardboard box, for the clothes moths cannot eat through paper. Moth balls keep the moths away, but do not kill the eggs or larvae which may already be present.

WHY DO MOSQUITO BITES ITCH?

Have you ever heard the expression, "The female of the species is deadlier than the male"? Well, it certainly applies to mosquitoes. Only female mosquitoes suck blood. The bill of the female has some sharp piercing organs, arranged around a sucking tube. When the mosquito bites, it injects a poisonous liquid into the blood. This poison causes the pain and itching and produces the swelling.

Next to its bite, the hum of the mosquito is probably most annoying. This hum is very important to the mosquito, however, for it is a sort of mating call. The males make a deep, low hum by vibrating their wings rapidly, while the females have a shriller note.

Mosquitoes are found all over the world. But wherever they may live, all species begin their lives somewhere in the water. The females deposit their eggs on the surface of ponds, in pools, in rain barrels, in the oases of deserts, even in tin cans. Each female lays from 40 to 400 eggs. These may be laid singly or in compact raftlike masses.

Within a week, small footless larvae hatch out. These larvae wriggle through the water so actively that they are usually called "wrigglers." Since they cannot breathe under water, they spend most of the time on the surface. There they take in air through the breathing tubes on their tails, and weave bits of animal and plant matter into their mouths with the feathery brushes on their heads.

As the wrigglers grow, they molt, or shed their skins. The fourth time they molt, they change into pupae. The pupae spend most of the time near the surface breathing through hornlike tubes on their backs. The pupae do not eat, but after a few days their skins split and the full-grown mosquitoes crawl out.

Adult mosquitoes usually live only a few weeks. In some species, there are 12 generations of mosquitoes during one year!

HOW DID DINOSAURS EVOLVE?

Scientists believe that dinosaurs came into being about 180,000,000 years ago and died out about 60,000,000 years ago. Since dinosaurs were reptiles, they must have developed from reptiles that lived before them. Reptiles, by the way, are a separate class of animals with these characteristics: They are cold-blooded; they can live on land; they have a distinctive type of heart; and most of them have scales.

The first reptiles appeared long before the dinosaurs. They looked like Amphibia (able to live in water and on land), but their eggs could be hatched on land. The young ones had legs and lungs, could breathe air, and probably ate insects.

Then the reptiles became larger and stronger. Some looked like big lizards and others like turtles. They had short tails, thick legs, and big heads. They ate plants.

The first dinosaurs to develop resembled their reptile ancestors, who were like lizards, and who could walk on their hindlegs. The first dinosaurs were slender, about as large as a turkey, and could also walk on their hindlegs. Some kinds remained small, but others grew heavier and longer. In time, many of them were six to eight feet long. There were even a few 20 feet long and weighing as much as an elephant. They had small heads and short, blunt teeth, which were only good for eating plants. They lived in low, swampy places.

Then came the next period in the Age of Reptiles. Some of the plant-eating dinosaurs became so large that even four legs couldn't support them on land. They had to spend most of their lives in rivers and swamps. One of these giants was Brontosaurus, 70 to 80 feet long and weighing about 38 tons!

At the same time, other dinosaurs were able to walk about on land. One of these, Allosaurus, was 34 feet long, had sharp teeth and claws, and fed on Brontosaurus and other plant-eaters! So dinosaurs were a stage in the development of the reptiles. They may have disappeared because of changes in the climate of the earth, which robbed them of places to wade and feed.

WHAT IS A VAMPIRE BAT?

When you think for what a short time man has existed on this earth, it is hard to believe that bats have existed for 60,000,000 years! There are fossil remains of bats going back to that time. There are even pictures of bats that are 4,000 years old, found in an Egyptian tomb.

Today there are several hundred different kinds of bats, and they live everywhere in the world except near the polar regions. Bats are the only mammals that can fly. They range in size from a six-inch wingspread to some that have almost a six-foot wingspread!

Most bats eat insects. Many bats of the warm tropics eat fruit or the pollen from flowers. Other bats eat fish or smaller bats. Some eat blood.

The blood-eating bats are called "vampire bats," and it is because of them that many people are so frightened of all bats. At one time, in Eastern Europe, there were many legends about vampires. A vampire was the soul of a dead person, which assumed the form of some animal at night, and roved the countryside looking for victims from which to suck blood. During

the early 18th century, explorers who traveled to South and Central America found bats that fed on blood. They came back with exaggerated stories, and soon, all the old vampire legends became associated with bats. Since that time, vampires have been thought of mostly as bats.

Vampire bats are found only in Central and South America. They have a wingspread of about 12 inches and a body length of about four inches. The vampire bat has needle-sharp front teeth with which it makes small cuts in the skin of its victim. At one time, it was thought a vampire bat sucked up the blood, but it actually laps it up with its tongue. In fact, a vampire bat can be feeding on its victim while the person remains sound asleep!

It is thought the saliva of the vampire bat contains some substance that deadens the pain of the wound, as well as something that prevents it from clotting. Vampire bats do not prefer to feed on human beings. They are just as happy to feed on horses, cows, goats, and chickens. In some places, vampire bats transmit a disease that is sometimes fatal to the victim.

HOW DOES A CHAMELEON CHANGE ITS COLORS?

How does the chameleon change its colors from a bright green to a grey-black or to yellow spots? Did nature give the chameleon an automatic color changer for its skin, so that it could resemble its background wherever it goes?

The strange fact about the chameleon's ability to change its colors is that it is not caused by the color of its surroundings! The chameleon pays no attention to its surroundings.

The skin of the chameleon is transparent. Underneath this skin, there are layers of cells which contain yellow, black, and red coloring matter. When these cells contract or expand, we see a change in the color of the chameleon.

But what makes those cells go to work? When the chameleon becomes angry or frightened, its nervous system sends a message to those cells. Anger cause the colors to darken; excitement and fright bring paler shades and yellow spots.

Sunlight also affects the chameleon's colors. Hot sunlight will make those cells turn dark, or almost black. High temperatures without sunlight usually produce green colors, low temperatures produce green colors. And darkness makes the chameleon fade to a cream color with yellow spots.

So we see that various things like emotion, temperature, and light cause the nervous system of the chameleon to make its color cells perform their tricks, and not the color of its surroundings.

It so happens, of course, that these changes in color help the chameleon become almost invisible to its enemies like snakes or birds. And because the chameleon is such a slow-moving animal, it needs this kind of protection to save its life.

WHY DOES A BULL CHARGE AT A RED CLOTH?

As you know, bullfighting is the greatest sport in Spain, and a very important one in many other countries. And people are quite excited about this sport. They believe certain things about it and nothing can change their minds.

One of the things most bullfight fans (and others) believe is that anything red makes a bull angry and causes him to attack. Therefore, the bullfighter has to have a bright red cape and he has to be able to use this with great skill.

Well, the sad truth is that if the same bullfighter had a white cloth, or a yellow cloth, or a green cloth, or a black cloth—he would be able to accomplish the same things with the bull! Bulls are color-blind!

Many bullfighters will privately admit they know this. In fact, some matadors conducted experiments in which they used white cloths—and they got the bulls to behave in the same way as with red cloths!

What makes the bull charge then? It is the movement of the cape, and not the color of it. Anything that you would wave in front of a bull would excite him. In fact, since the bull is color-blind, if you waved a white cape or cloth you would probably get a better reaction, since he can see it better!

DOES AN OSTRICH REALLY HIDE ITS HEAD IN THE SAND?

The ostrich is a rather strange bird, and there are many interesting and peculiar things about it, but it does not hide its head in the sand!

According to popular belief, when an ostrich is frightened it feels that it is safely hidden when it has its head in the sand. At such times, according to these stories, a person can walk up to the ostrich and capture it easily.

However, the truth is that no one has actually observed this happening! The ostrich simply does not hide its head in the sand. What may have given people the idea is that when an ostrich is frightened, it will sometimes drop to the ground, stretch out its neck parallel with it, and lie still and watch intently. But when the danger comes closer, the ostrich does just what other animals do—it takes off and runs!

The ostrich, of course, is one of the birds that cannot fly. But it makes up for this in its ability to run with considerable speed. The ostrich is the fastest-running bird in the world. It can go as fast as 50 miles an hour and is able to maintain this speed for at least a half-mile!

You sort of expect the ostrich to do everything on a large scale. The African ostrich, for example, is the largest living bird. No other bird even comes near it. This ostrich has been found to measure eight feet in height and to weigh more than 300 pounds. It would be some job carrying that weight around on a pair of wings, wouldn't it?

When it comes to eggs, the ostrich is champ again. It lays the largest eggs of any living bird. Ostrich eggs measure six to seven inches in length and five to six inches in diameter. It takes more than 40 minutes to boil an ostrich egg, if you happen to be thinking of having one for breakfast!

WHAT CAUSES THE SKUNK'S BAD SMELL?

If there is one animal in the world which you wouldn't want to be—it's probably a skunk. Yet the skunk is a friendly creature and makes a good pet. What makes him so unpopular, of course, is that famous smell of his.

What makes a skunk smell? The skunk has very powerful scent glands which contain a bad-smelling fluid. The skunk can send this fluid out with great accuracy.

The two glands are under the tail. A skunk aims at its enemy and shoots the liquid out in a spray. The spray can travel nine feet or more. The skunk may decide to send out spray from one gland or the other, or both, and each gland holds enough for five or six shots.

The spray is so strong that it has a suffocating effect, which means it makes it hard to breathe when you're near it. And if the spray gets into the eyes, it can cause temporary blindness!

But the skunk doesn't "strike" without warning. It raises its tail first or stamps its feet, so that you should have plenty of time to run away. Since skunks have been used for fur coats and are raised on fur farms, the scent glands, for obvious reasons, sometimes are removed from the young skunk.

There are actually three types of skunks, the striped, the hog-nosed, and the spotted. They live in North, Central, and South America. The striped skunk has a white line on the head from the nose to a point between the short ears, and another that starts on the neck, divides into two stripes on the back, and continues to the tail. Striped skunks live from Canada to Mexico. The largest are 2½ feet long, including the nine-inch tail, and weigh as much as 30 pounds.

The fore (front) feet of skunks are armed with long claws, which are used to dig grubs and insects out of the ground. When you see many shallow holes in the ground, it probably means a skunk has been feeding there.

Skunks are really a great help to man, since their food is mainly beetles, grasshoppers, crickets, wasps, rodents, and snakes.

CAN GROUNDHOGS PREDICT THE WEATHER?

Sometimes an idea is built up, or kept up, by newspapers because it "makes a good story." This seems to be the case with the groundhog and its ability to predict the weather.

The belief that the groundhog is a weather prophet is an old one. The groundhog, or woodchuck, or marmot, is a hibernating animal. It lives in a burrow during the winter months. According to an old tradition it comes out on the second day of February, which has come to be called "Groundhog Day."

Once the groundhog gets out of its burrow, it is supposed to look over the landscape. If the day is cloudy so that it can't see its shadow, it stays out. This is supposed to be a good sign. It means the weather will be mild for the rest of the winter. But if the groundhog sees its shadow because the day is clear, it goes back into its burrow to get some more sleep. According to tradition, this means there will be six more weeks of cold weather.

The reason I say that newspapers seem to try to keep up the tradition is that it always makes a good story, and this despite the fact that most people don't really believe it. To begin with, there is absolutely no reason why the groundhog should be able to predict the weather. It has no special ability of any kind.

Another reason is that the groundhog doesn't really come out of its burrow on the second of February every year. Sometimes it comes out earlier, sometimes later. Occasionally a newspaperman will force the poor groundhog out on the right day in order to take pictures. But obviously, if the weather is still very cold, the groundhog has no desire at all to emerge from its warm burrow.

The tradition is said to have originated in Europe concerning the hedgehog. But the Pilgrims transferred it to the groundhog when they came to this country.

WHY DOES THE KANGAROO HAVE A POUCH?

Animals that have a pouch (and the kangaroo is only one of several animals like this) are called "marsupials."

The pouch that the kangaroo has, which is between her hindlegs, is about as snug and comfortable a little home as a new-born baby can have. It is fur-lined, keeps the baby warm, protects it, enables the baby to nurse, and provides transportation for the helpless infant.

The reason a pouch is provided by nature for kangaroos and other marsupials is that their young are born in a very helpless state. In fact, at birth the kangaroo is a tiny, pink, naked mass, not much over an inch long and as thick as a lead pencil! Can you imagine what would happen if such a helpless thing didn't immediately have a place to keep it warm, snug, and protected?

The mother places the new-born baby in the pouch and for six months this is "home." In six months, the young kangaroo is as large as a puppy. But life is too good in the pouch to leave home. So "the joey," as it is called in Australia, rides around inside the pouch with its head sticking out far enough for it to pull off leaves when its mother stops to feed on tree branches, In fact, even after the mother has taught it how to walk and run, the joey still lives in the pouch. In case of danger, the mother hops over to it, picks it up in her mouth without stopping, and drops it safely into her pouch.

There are more than 120 different kinds of kangaroos. The wallaby, which is the smallest, is only two feet high. The biggest is the great red or gray kangaroo, which is about six feet tall!

Kangaroos have short front legs with small paws, and very long hind-legs with one large sharp toe in the middle of the foot. With the help of its powerful hindlegs, a kangaroo takes jumps of 10 to 15 feet or more. When the kangaroo is resting, it rests on its big, long tail. Kangaroos can travel very fast, and their sense of hearing is so good they can hear an enemy at a great distance.

WHY DOES THE GIRAFFE HAVE A LONG NECK?

Giraffes have aroused the curiosity of man since earliest times. The ancient Egyptians and Greeks had a theory that giraffes were a mixture of the leopard and the camel, and they called the giraffe "a camelopard."

The giraffe is the tallest of all living animals, but scientists are unable to explain how it got its long neck. A famous French zoologist, Jean Baptiste de Lamarck, had a theory that at one time the giraffe's neck was much shorter than it now is. He thought that the neck grew to its present length because of the animal's habit of reaching for the tender leaves in the upper branches of trees. But scientists in general don't accept de Lamarck's theory.

Strangely enough, the body of a giraffe is no larger than that of the average horse. Its tremendous height, which may reach 20 feet, comes mostly from its legs and neck. The neck of a giraffe has only seven vertebrae, which is what the human neck has. But each vertebra is extremely long. Because of this, a giraffe always has a stiff neck. If it wants to take a drink from the ground, it has to spread its legs far apart in order to be able to reach down!

The strange shape and build of the giraffe is perfectly suited to enable it to obtain its food. A giraffe eats only plants, so its great height enables it to reach the leaves on trees which grow in tropical lands where there is little grass.

A giraffe's tongue is often a foot and a half long, and it can use it so skillfully that it can pick the smallest leaves off thorny plants without being pricked. It also has a long upper lip which helps it wrench off many leaves at a time.

The giraffe is able to protect itself from danger in many ways. First of all, the coloring of its hide makes it practically invisible when it is feeding in the shadows of trees. It has well-developed ears which are sensitive to the faintest sounds, and it has keen senses of smell and sight. Finally, a giraffe can gallop at more than 30 miles an hour when pursued and can outrun the fastest horse!

When attacked, a giraffe can put up a good fight by kicking out with its hindlegs or using its head like a sledge hammer. Even a lion is careful in attacking a giraffe, always approaching it from behind!

CHAPTER 5
HOW THINGS ARE MADE

WHAT IS A MAGNET?

There is an old legend that a shepherd called Magnes, tending his flocks along the slopes of Mount Ida, discovered that his iron crook and the iron nails of his sandals were clinging to a large black stone. The fact that certain stones could attract iron was the discovery of magnetism. These mysterious stones were also found near a place called Magnesia in Asia Minor. The name "magnet" may have been created for either of these reasons.

As time went by, a further discovery was made about magnetism. It was found that when pieces of iron were rubbed against the magnetic stones, they also became magnets. Thousands of years ago it was also discovered that a suspended magnet would point approximately to the north. This, of course, was the creation of the compass. The magnetic stones were called "lodestone." The name comes from "leading stone," because they helped guide the wanderer.

In Queen Elizabeth's time it was first discovered that every magnet has two definite poles, which are opposite in nature. Like poles repel each other, and unlike poles attract.

Nothing much was done about magnetism until the beginning of the 19th century. In 1820, Oersted, a Danish scientist, discovered that a wire carrying an electric current also created a magnetic field. This led to the discovery that by putting soft-iron core inside wires that were connected to a battery, the iron core became magnetized. It was the first creation of the electromagnet, much more powerful than any magnets ever known before.

The creation of the electromagnet made possible many of the most important and useful instruments we now have. Not only do electromagnets lift great weights, but they play a part in bells and buzzers, dynamos and motors, in fact, in anything that uses an electrical circuit.

Although it had long been known that the force of a magnet reaches out some distance from the magnet, Michael Faraday was the first one to define and show "the fields of force" and "lines of force." The understanding of this made possible such developments as the telephone, the electric light, the radio, and so on.

HOW DOES A SEISMOGRAPH RECORD EARTHQUAKES?

Sometimes there is a big news story about an earthquake that happened in some distant part of the world, perhaps in South America or Japan. You read and hear about cities being destroyed, hundreds of people being killed. Yet you, in your home, felt nothing! If the earth "shook," why didn't you feel it where you live?

Well, maybe you didn't feel it—but not far from you, in a big city or university, scientists probably made a complete and exact record of that earthquake! They felt it on their instruments.

Such an instrument is called "a seismograph." In fact, the study of earthquakes is known as "seismology." Now let's see why you didn't feel it and the scientists were able to make a record of it.

An earthquake is a trembling or vibration of the earth's surface. Notice the word "surface." That means just the crust of the earth. An earthquake is usually caused by a "fault" in the rocks of the earth's crust—a break along which one rock mass has rubbed on another with very great force and friction. The energy of this rubbing is changed to vibration in the rocks. And this vibration may travel thousands of miles.

Now these earthquake vibrations are a kind of wave motion which travels at different speeds through the earth's rocky crust. Because they have such a long distance to go, and are traveling through rock, by the time they reach your town you can't even notice them. But the seismograph can. This is how it works.

Imagine a block or slab of concrete. Sticking out of this slab is a chart that is fixed to it. It is parallel to the ground, like a sheet of paper. Above it, a rod sticks out from which is hung a weight. At the bottom of the weight is a pen, which touches the chart. Now comes an earthquake wave. The concrete block moves and the chart with it. But the weight, which is suspended, doesn't move. So the pen makes markings on the chart as it moves and we get a record of the earthquakes. Of course, this instrument is arranged very delicately so the slightest motion will be recorded.

WHAT IS PENICILLIN?

Few weapons against disease created as much excitement and became well-known as quickly as penicillin. It was as if suddenly the whole world became aware of a "miracle" happening before its eyes.

Yet penicillin is not one of man's miracles, created by a genius in a laboratory. It is one of nature's own miracles. Penicillin is the name we give to a powerful substance which fights bacteria and which is developed by certain moulds. It is an "antibiotic," which means a substance produced by a living organism and which acts upon other harmful organisms or bacteria.

Oddly enough, the whole idea of antibiotics is not a new one. As far back as 1877, antibiotic action was discovered by Louis Pasteur, and various antibiotic substances were used to treat infections. In fact, moulds and fungi themselves were used to treat infections, and it is quite probable that even a penicillin-producing mould was used against infection many years ago, but no one knew what it was!

In 1928, Sir Alexander Fleming was the first to describe and name this strange substance "penicillin." It was discovered almost by accident, but it soon became the subject of intensive study. It was found that certain moulds produced this substance which had a powerful and destructive effect on many of the common bacteria which infect man, while it had no effect on many others.

Something else very important was discovered about penicillin. While it could act so powerfully against bacteria, it did not have a harmful effect on human cells. This was important because all the other antiseptics in common use had a greater effect on human cells than they did on harmful bacteria!

Penicillin is very selective in its action. This means that it has a powerful effect on some bacteria and little or none on others. It is not an all-around drug used to kill any kind of bacteria, as some people believe.

Penicillin has three different kinds of effect on bacteria. It is "bacteriostatic," which means it stops the growth of bacteria. It is "bactericidal," which means it kills bacteria. And in some cases it even dissolves away the bacteria altogether!

HOW DOES A BATTERY PRODUCE ELECTRICITY?

There are two ways of producing electric current for power. It can be produced by machines called "dynamos," or "generators"—and by battery cells.

A battery cell produces electricity by changing chemical energy into electrical energy. Part of the chemical energy is changed into heat and part of it into an electric current.

There are two kinds of battery cells. One, called "a primary cell," cannot be renewed when it's used except by replenishing its chemicals. The ordinary dry cell (such as in your flashlight) is a primary cell. The other type, called "a secondary cell," can be recharged by sending an electric current through it. The storage cells used to start automobiles are secondary cells.

A battery is a group of two or more primary or secondary cells. A single cell is often called "a battery," but this isn't correct.

Various chemicals are used in primary cells, but the principle is always the same. In every primary cell there are electrodes and an electrolyte. The electrodes, or "cell elements" as they are called, have two different metals or one metal and carbon. The electrolyte is a liquid.

One of the elements, called "the cathode," is usually zinc. The other is called "the anode," and is usually carbon. Chemical action causes the cathode to dissolve slowly in the electrolyte. This sets electrons free. Now if a path, or circuit, is provided through which these free electrons can move, they provide an electric current. When you connect the elements by a wire or other electrical conductor, the current flows through it and you have "electricity."

A storage battery does not really store electricity. It obtains its power from chemical changes, just as all other kinds do. One set of plates in a storage battery is made of metallic lead and the other of lead peroxide. Both sets are immersed in sulphuric acid, and both gradually change to lead sulphate. It is this chemical process which produces the electric current in a storage battery.

HOW DOES AN ELECTRIC BULB GIVE LIGHT?

In 1800, an Englishman called Humphry Davy was conducting certain experiments with electricity. He had what we now call an electric battery, but it was quite weak. He connected wires to the ends of the battery and attached a piece of carbon to each of the free ends of the wires. By touching the two pieces of carbon together and drawing them slightly apart, he produced a sizzling light.

This was called "an electric arc," but it was the first evidence that electric light is possible. Davy also replaced the two pieces of carbon by a thin platinum wire connecting the two ends of the wires leading to the battery. When the electric current passed through it, the wire was heated and began to glow and gave light!

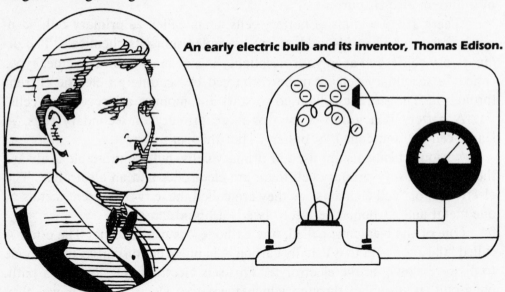

An early electric bulb and its inventor, Thomas Edison.

The trouble with these simple electric lights was that the source of electricity wasn't strong enough. So a pupil of Davy's, Michael Faraday, conducted experiments that led to the development of electric generators. By using steam engines to drive the generators, better sources of electricity were found.

Meanwhile, in the United States, Thomas Edison was experimenting with thin threads of carbon. When the carbon thread, or filament, was heated by passing electric current through it, it glowed. If this was done in air, the carbon itself would burn. So Edison placed it in a glass bulb and pumped out the air. Because there was no oxygen in the bulb, the carbon couldn't burn. It glowed brightly and only wasted away very slowly. Now we had an electric bulb that gave pretty good light.

But scientists knew that the more a filament is heated, the more light it gives. So they looked for materials that could be heated to high temperatures without melting. One of these is tantalum, a metal that melts at a temperature of 5,160 degrees Fahrenheit. It was drawn into fine wires and used for lamp filaments in 1905.

An even better metal for the filament is tungsten, because it melts at 6,100 degrees Fahrenheit. At first no one could draw tungsten into wire, and it took years to develop this process. Today, tungsten-filament lamps are the ones most widely used of all, and about 1,000,000,000 of them are made in the United States each year!

WHAT MAKES FLUORESCENT LIGHTS WORK?

Most things that can be made to glow will do so only when they are hot. In the ordinary light bulbs, for example, there is a filament that must be heated to high temperature in order to give off light.

But there are also many materials which can glow in different colors without being hot. They give off this glow when invisible ultraviolet rays fall upon them. These invisible rays "excite" the materials, and the giving-off of light that results is called "fluorescence."

The word "fluorescence" comes from the name of the mineral "fluor-spar," which can fluoresce in different colors. Some materials will fluoresce only when they are a gas, others when a liquid, and still others as a solid material. The most important ones are solid crystal powders which are called "phosphors."

How does fluorescence come about? The first thing that must happen is that the "exciting" rays which fall on the fluorescent material must be absorbed by it. Now, these rays are really a form of energy. So certain atoms within the materials take in some of this energy and become "excited." After a very short time in this excited state, they return again to their natural, original state. During this return, they give off the extra energy they have absorbed in the form of light. This is called "fluorescence."

How do fluorescent lamps work? Mercury vapor is put into a long glass tube. Then an electric current is passed through this tube. This produces ultraviolet rays. The inside wall of the lamp is coated with a phosphor, and this phosphor absorbs all the ultraviolet rays. It becomes "excited," as we have just described. It thus gives off light!

By means of fluorescence, about four times as much white light can be produced as by ordinary incandescent lamps. Fluorescent lamps last ten times as long as ordinary incandescent lamps. They can also be made in various shapes. Because of these advantages, fluorescent lighting is being used more and more in homes, schools, stores, and factories.

WHAT IS GASOLINE?

Why is gasoline a perfect fuel? It's a liquid, it is light, it easily changes into vapor, and it is easily ignited.

Gasoline is a mixture of hydrocarbons, which means it is a compound made up of carbon and hydrogen. The name "gasoline" comes from "gas." It is used because the liquid gasoline is so easily changed into a gas in the cylinder. Once gasoline is ignited, it burns almost completely and leaves very little waste. In burning, it gives more heat than the same amount of any other liquid fuel.

Where does gasoline come from? There are several sources, but the most important is natural crude oil, or petroleum, which is found in deposits under the ground. Gasoline is separated from petroleum by a process called "distillation." The liquid oil is placed in large containers, called "stills," and heated to about 400 degrees Fahrenheit. This is just enough to change into vapor about one quarter of the petroleum containing the hydrocarbons that boil lowest.

The vapor is led through pipes cooled from the outside so that it becomes a liquid again (is condensed). The distillation is repeated, and the gasoline is purified, or refined.

The value of a gasoline depends on its performance; that is, how many miles a gallon will drive a car or fly a plane at high speed. With simple, refined gasoline we hear knocking sounds in the motor. When a gasoline knocks, its performance is poor, because it is igniting poorly. So certain "anti-knock" ingredients are added which make it perform better. We call this "high-octane" gasoline. Today, better and better grades of high-octane gasoline are being produced to give our cars better performance.

HOW DOES GASOLINE MAKE AN AUTOMOBILE RUN?

Today cars are built so efficiently that people can drive all their life without really knowing what makes them run! We just pull up to a gasoline station, fill up the tank, and away we go. If anything goes wrong, a service man fixes it for us.

Now, all of us know that the power to drive the automobile motor comes from the gasoline, but just how does this happen? It isn't very complicated, so let's trace it step by step.

The gasoline is delivered from the fuel tank in the car to the engine by means of a small pump driven by the engine. The gasoline first goes into the carburetor on top of the engine. Here it is thoroughly mixed with exactly the right amount of air.

We now have a gasoline-air vapor which is highly explosive. It next passes through a system of pipes (called "a manifold") on its way into the cylinder. In the cylinder there is a piston and as it moves down in the cylinder it sucks the gasoline-air vapor into the engine. This is the first stroke of what is known as "the four-stroke cycle."

As soon as the piston reaches the bottom of its stroke, a valve closes so that none of the vapor can escape. When the piston moves upward on its second stroke, it squeezes the trapped vapor, making it even more explosive. At just the right moment, when the piston reaches the top of its second stroke, an electric spark is created by the spark plug and this sets off the vapor.

The pressure caused by the explosion forces the piston down again on the third stroke. When the piston reaches the bottom of its third stroke, another valve opens to let the burned gases escape, and they are pushed out as the piston rises on its fourth and final stroke.

The power for the car comes from the third, or power, stroke. The forces pressing downward on the top of the piston are transmitted to the crankshaft to make it turn, and the turning driveshaft drives the rear wheels.

HOW DOES A JET ENGINE WORK?

Although jet engines power the newest, most powerful aircraft we have today, the principle behind them was discovered about 2,000 years ago! That principle is jet propulsion, and it was first shown by a Greek mathematician, Hero of Alexander, in about 120 B.C. He used the force of steam escaping from a heated metal ball to spin the ball like a wheel.

To show how jet propulsion works, let's consider an ordinary blown-up balloon. When the balloon's mouth is closed, the air inside pushes in all directions with the same force. When the mouth is opened, the air pressure is lessened at that place as the air rushes out. However, at the top of the balloon, the point opposite the mouth, the air pushes with greater pressure. The balloon then moves in the direction of the greatest pressure, which is forward. So it is not the exhaust (air rushing out) but the forward push which causes the balloon to move.

This is because there is a law of motion as follows: To every action there is an equal and opposite reaction. In a jet engine, the "action" is the exhaust's backward push, while the equal and opposite "reaction" is the forward thrust.

There are two basic types of jet engines: ramjets and turbojets. The ramjet is like a flying stovepipe. It has no moving parts. Air is forced into the front opening, called "the intake," by its own forward motion. The air is then mixed with fuel and burned, increasing the gas about five times in volume. It is then exhausted through the smaller tail end. The fire in a ramjet creates no push when standing still, but the faster it moves, the more power it produces.

In a turbojet, air is sucked in by a compressor. It is then compressed and forced into the combustion chamber where it is mixed with fuel and burned. The hot, expanded gases go through a turbine and then escape through the exhaust nozzle, producing jet thrust. If the energy is delivered to the turbine, and the turbine shaft is made to turn the propeller of the airplane, we have a jet engine that is called "a turboprop."

HOW DOES A SUBMARINE STAY UNDER WATER?

The basic principle that enables a submarine to submerge or to surface is a very simple one. Most modern submarines have two hulls, or bodies. Water ballast is stowed between the inner and outer hulls, which might be considered similar to "shells."

When a submarine is ready to submerge, large valves known as "kingstons," located at the bottom of the ballast tanks, are opened to let in the sea. The air in the tanks escapes through valves at the top, known as "vents." The submarine goes under water!

When a submarine is ready to surface, the vents are closed and air pressure is forced into the tanks. This blows the water back out through the kingstons, and the submarine rises.

To guide the submarine in diving and rising, there are horizontal rudders fitted to the hull. To steer the submarine when it is moving forward. there is a rudder just like on surface-type ships.

A submarine is divided by crosswise bulkheads, or walls, into compartments. To go from one compartment into another, one has to pass through watertight, quick-closing doors. Submarines have escape hatches and safety lungs for emergency use.

How does a submarine know where it's going? Observation is done by means of a periscope, which consists of a long tube that can be pushed up from inside the vessel. By use of a combination of prisms, someone who is at the lower end of the periscope can see objects on the surface. By revolving the periscope tube, he can sweep the entire ocean horizon.

Submarines also have listening devices which can pick up and locate the sound of distant ships, and radar which enables them to find objects when they are on the surface.

In 1951, the world's first atomic submarine was ordered built, and it was launched on July 21, 1955.

HOW IS CHEWING GUM MADE?

Chewing gum is made of a gum base, sugar, corn sirup, and flavoring. The gum base is what keeps it chewy for hours. Bubble gum is made with a more rubbery gum base so that it will stretch without tearing.

Each manufacturer has his own recipe which is very secret, but the method of manufacturing the gum is more or less the same for all. At the factory, the gum base is prepared. The materials are melted and sterilized in a steam cooker and pumped through a centrifuge. This machine spins at high speed and throws out dirt and bits of bark found in the raw gums.

The clean, melted gum base is mixed with sugar, corn sirup, and flavoring. The usual mixture is 20 per cent gum base, 63 per cent sugar,

16 per cent corn sirup, and about 1 per cent flavoring oils. Some of the more popular flavors are spearmint, peppermint, clove, and cinnamon.

While this mass is still warm, it is run between pairs of rollers. These thin it down into a long ribbon. Powdered sugar on both sides prevents the gum from sticking. The last pair of rollers is fitted with knives which cut the ribbon into sticks. Machines wrap the sticks separately and then into packages.

Most of the gum base that is now used is manufactured, that is, it's a product of industry. But some of it, like chicle, comes from trees. Chicle comes from the wild sapodilla tree of Guatemala and Mexico.

The milky white sap of this tree is collected in buckets. Then it is boiled down and molded into 25-pound blocks to be shipped to chewing gum factories.

People in Central America chew chicle right from the tree. In the same way, early New England settlers chewed spruce gum, after seeing the Indians do it. This was the first gum sold in the United States in the early 1800's. Chicle was first imported in the 1860's as a substitute for rubber. Then, about 1890, it began to be used in making chewing gum, and from then on our modern chewing gum industry became established.

WHAT MAKES CORN POP?

As far as most children are concerned, the most amazing thing about corn is its ability to "pop." The explanation is very simple. Popcorn kernels are small and very hard. When they are heated, the moisture within the hard shells turns to steam and explodes!

But that's only the beginning of all the wonders of corn. It is really one of the most remarkable plants known to man. Here is just a rough idea of the ways in which corn products can be used. Corn starch is used on stamps and envelopes; corn oil is used in food, and in making paints, rubber substitutes, and soap. Alcohol is made from corn; smokeless powder and guncotton are made from the corn stalk and so is paper. Even cloth and ink can be made from the corn cob!

This amazing plant, which belongs to the grass family, grows in six general types. Dent corn is distinguished by the fact that when dried, the upper part of the kernel becomes indented. Flint corn has very hard kernels and long, slender ears. Soft corn grows in the Southern United States and has very soft kernels. Sweet corn is the type used for canning or eating directly from the cob. Popcorn is the kind that explodes when heated, and pod corn has each kernel enclosed in a tiny husk of its own.

Originally, the word "corn" meant a small, hard particle of something. It usually referred to the hard seed of a plant. In Europe, the word "corn" is still applied to different grains. In Scotland it means oats, in northern Europe rye, and in other countries wheat and barley. Europeans call our corn "maize," which was its original Indian name.

Three-quarters of all the corn grown in the world is grown in the United States, and that amounts to about 2,500,000,000 bushels a year! In fact, if we could load our annual crop of corn into wagons of average size, a procession of them would reach around the world almost six times. It is by far America's most important farm crop.

Today, of course, the cultivation of corn is carried on along scientific lines and the development of new and better types of corn is going on all the time. Yet even before Columbus discovered America, the Indians were cultivating corn with their simple methods and it was the main source of food for many of the tribes!

WHAT IS DRY ICE?

If liquid carbon dioxide is cooled to a certain temperature and subjected to pressure, it forms a white solid that looks like snow. This is called "Dry Ice." More than a hundred years ago, scientists had succeeded in making solid carbon dioxide. In this form it was like snow, and it produced temperatures as low as 109 degrees below zero Fahrenheit. It was then seen that solid carbon dioxide could be very useful for refrigerating purposes, but chemists weren't able to control it because when it melted it turned into a liquid.

When solid carbon dioxide was mixed with liquids like alcohol, which have very low freezing temperatures, the problem was solved. The trademark name "Dry Ice" is used because the solid material doesn't melt into a liquid but turns into gas. This is very convenient because the gas escapes into the air. Solid carbon dioxide, or Dry Ice, gives more refrigeration than the same amount of water ice.

The first important use for solid carbon dioxide was for packing ice cream. Now fish, meat, and other perishable products are shipped thousands of miles and kept in perfect condition with this material. Eggs refrigerated with solid carbon dioxide remain fresh almost indefinitely. This is because eggs grow stale when carbon dioxide escapes through the pores of the shell. When they are refrigerated with carbon dioxide, a vapor of the gas surrounds the eggs, and they remain fresh! Florists can keep rosebuds from opening for three days when they are kept in an atmosphere of carbon dioxide!

HOW IS SUGAR MADE?

Sugar is one of the oldest products man has been able to make from nature. Thousands of years ago, the people of India learned how to make sugar from sugar cane. But Europe didn't even know such a thing existed until the Arabs introduced it at the time of the Crusades. At first sugar was considered a rarity and was even used as a medicine.

Today, sugar is a relatively cheap food. In the United States, the average person consumes about 100 pounds of sugar every year! By the word "sugar" today, we may be describing any of over 100 sweet-tasting substances, but each has the same chemical composition. It consists of three elements, carbon, hydrogen, and oxygen. While the amount of carbon may vary, there is always twice as much hydrogen as oxygen, which makes sugar a carbohydrate.

Sugar is made by plants for their own use. This sugar is stored away in the plant until it is needed to make seeds and fiber or material for growth. As a food for man, sugar supplies heat and energy and helps to form fat.

The various kinds of sugar come from widely different sources. Milk sugar, or lactose, which is used for babies, comes from milk. From fruit we get a sugar called "fructose." From vegetables, grain, potatoes, we get glucose. The most common sugar, sucrose, comes chiefly from beets and sugar cane.

Sugar cane is a member of the grass family. It grows in the warm, moist climate of the tropics and subtropics, and sometimes reaches a height of 20 feet. When the stalks of the sugar cane have been cut, they are trimmed and taken to the cane mill or sugar factory. There they are washed and cut into short lengths or shredded. The rough pulpy mass is then crushed between heavy rollers.

The liquid pressed out of the cane is a dark grayish or greenish color and is acid. Since this contains impurities, it is necessary to use chemicals to clear it up. The clear juice is then run into vacuum pans and evaporated into a thick sirup, which is a mixture of sugar crystals and molasses. This is revolved in hollow cylinders to force out the molasses sirup, leaving the raw, brown sugar inside. This brown sugar then goes to a refinery, where it is dissolved, treated with chemicals, filtered, and finally it is crystallized again. Now we have pure white sugar, which is then made into granulated, lump, or powdered form.

WHERE DOES STARCH COME FROM?

More food for the human race is furnished by starch than is gained from any other single substance! This alone would make starch one of the most important substances in the world. But, of course, starch has many other uses, too, ranging from adhesives and laundering to use as a basis in many toilet preparations.

Starch is produced by plants and in the plants it is found in the form of tiny grains. With the help of sunshine and chlorophyll (the green matter in their leaves), plants combine water from the soil and the carbon dioxide from the air into sugar.

This sugar is changed by the plants into starch. The starch is stored away as small granules in large quantities in their stems, roots, leaves, fruits, and seeds. The white potato, for example, contains large amounts of starch. Such cereals as corn, rice, and wheat also contain large quantities.

Why do the plants store away starch? It serves as food for the development of seedlings or the new shoots until they can manufacture their own food materials.

For men and animals, starch supplies an energy-producing food. Like sugar, it is made up of carbon, hydrogen, and oxygen. It is not sweet; generally, it is tasteless.

Starch is obtained from a plant by crushing the plant tissue which contains the starch. The starch is washed out with water and allowed to settle to the bottom of large vats. The water is then squeezed out of the wet starch and the mass is dried and ground to a powder.

Some of the most common sources of starch are white potatoes, sweet potatoes, the grain crops, arrowroot, the sago palm, and the cassava plant of tropical America.

HOW DOES YEAST MAKE BREAD RISE?

Thousands of years ago, the Egyptians discovered that it was the yeast which made bread rise and so they were the first people to produce a "yeast-raised" bread. What is yeast, and how is it able to produce those light loaves of bread we enjoy today?

Yeast is a one-celled plant, so small that it cannot be seen without a microscope. But we can see yeast because it grows in colonies, made up of many yeast plants growing together. A yeast colony is almost colorless. It is not green because it has no chlorophyll. This is why yeast is called a "fungus." It cannot produce food for itself.

As yeast plants grow and reproduce, they form two substances called "enzymes," invertase and zymase. These enzymes help to convert (change) starch to sugar and sugar to alcohol, carbon dioxide, and energy.

This energy-producing process is called "fermentation." The carbon dioxide formed is a gas which man may use in a number of ways; one of them in making bread rise.

Years ago breadmakers found that bread would rise, or become light and fluffy, if allowed to stand for a time before baking. This happened because yeast plants from the air entered the dough and began to grow.

Today breadmakers add yeast and sugar to the dough as they make it. The starch and sugar in the bread dough serve as food for the yeast. Carbon dioxide is given off and forms bubbles inside the loaf. Heat from the oven causes the gas to expand. This makes the bread rise even more. Finally the heat drives off the carbon dioxide, and it leaves a light, dry loaf.

Yeast is grown in large vats, strained, mixed with starch, and pressed into cakes. It is then ready to be sold.

If yeast grows in a sugar solution, the carbon dioxide escapes but the alcohol stays in the solution. Whiskey, beer, ale, wine, and other alcoholic beverages are made in this way from fruit juices or grain mashes, such as rye, wheat, or corn.

WHAT IS CAFFEINE?

Today there is hardly a home in the Western world where coffee isn't found. So the effects of coffee and caffeine are of interest to a great many people. But did you know that coffee wasn't introduced into Europe until the latter part of the 17th century? Coffee was first known to the Abyssinians in eastern Africa, and for a period of 200 years all the world's coffee came from Yemen in southern Arabia.

The roasted coffee bean contains many substances, and the best known of these is caffeine. It is a substance chemically related to uric acid. Caffeine is not found in a free state, but combined with acids. A coffee bean contains about one per cent caffeine.

The effects produced by drinking coffee are not due only to the caffeine, but caffeine is the strongest of the substances in coffee. By the way, tea also contains caffeine, but the same amount of caffeine in tea has a different effect than when in coffee. The reason is that in each case the caffeine is combined with different substances. Also, if you add milk or cream to coffee, the caffeine combines with the protein of the milk, and its action is weakened.

What is the effect of coffee on the body? Surprisingly enough, it has not one effect but many. Coffee dilates the vessels in the brain and improves circulation there. It stimulates the nerve cells. It also increases the work done by the heart. (You can see how for some people this would not be desirable.) Coffee works on the movement of the intestine, and so has a mild laxative action.

Coffee also makes the gastric glands secrete more juices, and for some people this produces "heartburn," while for others it helps digestion. Altogether, coffee acts as a stimulant to the body and nerves. This is why some people complain that it "keeps them up" at night.

Generally speaking, drinking coffee is a matter of individual decision. People who are used to it, find it helps them feel better. Nervous people are apt to be injured by it. And, of course, people who drink it to excess may find it quite upsetting. But isn't that true of anything we eat or drink?

WHY IS MILK PASTEURIZED?

Since milk is such an important food, it has to be kept clean, sweet, and free from harmful bacteria. Pasteurization is only one of the many steps that are taken to provide you with safe, healthful milk. Let's see what happens to milk as it goes from the cow to your kitchen.

To begin with, the farmer sees that his cows receive several tests at regular intervals to make sure they are healthy. He also takes care to hire only healthy people to help him in handling milk.

Milking machines and milk pails are kept perfectly clean. As soon as each cow is milked, the milk is carried to the milkhouse where it is weighed, filtered, and cooled to the right temperature in preparation for shipment. Most farmers put their milk into 10-gallon steel cans which are smooth inside and have been well-tinned to prevent corrosion.

When milk has to be shipped to a city milk plant, it travels in milk tanks that are made of steel and highly insulated. A milk tank is like a huge thermos bottle. Even if the shipment is a long one, the insulation is so good that the temperature of the milk changes only one or two degrees!

When the milk arrives at the city milk plant, it is pumped into large holding tanks. Here the temperature is checked again and so is the odor. Other tests are made to assure the quality and sanitary condition of the milk.

Then the milk is pasteurized. This means that the milk is heated to a temperature at which any harmful bacteria which may be in the milk are killed. The process is named after the famous French scientist, Louis Pasteur, who developed it.

There are two methods of pasteurization. In one method, the milk is heated to a temperature of at least 143 degrees Fahrenheit for not less than 30 minutes. This is called the long-time, holding method. In the other method, the milk is heated to at least 160 degrees Fahrenheit and is held at that temperature for not less than 15 seconds. This is the short-time method. After pasteurization, the milk is cooled very rapidly.

Every step involved in the handling of milk is done with great care to make sure that the milk you drink is as clean and healthy as can be!

WHAT IS ALUMINUM?

Aluminum is one of the most abundant metals found in nature. It makes up nearly 8 per cent of the earth's crust. The trouble is that aluminum is never found free in nature, but in combination with various substances, it forms part of many rocks and soils.

The problem that science tackled, therefore, was how to make this metal cheaply and in large quantities. On February 23, 1886, a 22-year-old chemist called Charles Martin Hall solved the problem and a new metal age was born—the age of aluminum.

What he did was to melt cryolite, an aluminum compound, mix it with aluminum oxide, and then pass a direct electric current through the mixture. After a while, little "buttons" of metallic aluminum appeared, the first process ever discovered for producing the metal!

Metallic aluminum is a silvery-white, lustrous metal that is only about one-third as heavy as iron. It can be drawn out into wires that are finer than the finest hairs, and hammered out into sheets many times thinner than the paper in this book.

While certain acids will affect it, under ordinary conditions aluminum does not corrode. And when certain other metals are mixed with it, the resulting combinations, called "alloys," are stronger, harder, or tougher than aluminum itself!

Aluminum got its big start in the kitchen only because one of the first articles cast in this metal was a teapot! Of course it's an almost perfect material for cooking utensils because it conducts heat so well and is so easy to keep clean and bright. But its light weight makes it useful for things that range from electric cables to automobile engines. One of aluminum's greatest contributions to modern life has been its use in bodies, wings, and propellers of airplanes. Today, even railway engines use aluminum alloys!

Every year new uses for this metal are discovered. Ground up into a fine powder, it is mixed with oils and used as paint. It is used as a wrapper in the form of foil for soaps, cheese, cigarettes. Many of the tubes used for tooth paste, shaving creams, and so on, are made from aluminum. And now aluminum has found its way into furniture, buildings, toasters, radios, washing machines—into practically every part of our life!

HOW IS STAINLESS STEEL MADE?

Of all the alloys made, steel is one of the most important. Millions of tons are produced every year and it is used in a tremendous variety of products, from tools to rails.

Now, when other elements in addition to carbon are added to iron, the steel that results is called "an alloy steel." One of the most important alloy steels is stainless steel.

It was discovered that when in addition to the carbon and iron combination, about 10 to 20 per cent of chromium and some nickel was included, the result was a steel that resists rust, oxidation, and the attack of many acids.

Stainless steel then is steel with the addition of chromium and possibly some nickel. The use of stainless steel now extends to hundreds of products we come in contact with every day. It is used for table and kitchen knives, golf-club heads, door knobs, light fixtures, fishing gear—the list could go on and on.

Because stainless steel can take a high polish, it is often used for mirrors and reflectors where glass would be too brittle.

HOW DOES A CAMERA TAKE PICTURES?

The human eye is actually a form of camera. When you look around, your eyes "take pictures" of the things you see. The lens in your eye acts just like the lens in a camera. The retina of your eye acts like the film in your camera.

In your eye, the light acts on the sensitive surface of the retina. In a camera, light acts on a specially prepared sensitive surface of the film. If light didn't have an affect on certain chemically prepared substances, photography would be impossible.

What is this action? It is simply the fact that light makes the chemical silver nitrate turn black. Most photographic processes depend on this reaction, as we will now see.

The first problem is to focus the light on the sensitive material of the film. This is done by the lens of the camera, which collects and bends the light to form the picture. A lens is like "a light funnel" through which the light is directed onto the film.

When we open and close the shutter of the camera quickly, light comes in and strikes the film. When this happens, a chemical reaction takes place on the film. Certain tiny grains of silver bromide undergo a change. When this film is taken out of the camera and treated with various liquids, these grains, which have been affected by the light, turn up as the dark part of the film.

The more intense the light, the darker or denser is the patch it makes on the film. This film is called "a negative" because it has the opposite values of the picture. Dark parts of the scene you photographed look light, light parts look dark.

When the negative is ready, the next step is to make a "positive" print. The negative is placed against a special printing paper, which also is affected by light. So it is exposed to a bright light through the negative. The dark parts of the negative let less light go through to the printing paper, so those parts of the print will look light. In this way, we get again the values of the original subject we photographed. The picture that comes out on the printing paper thus has gone through a negative stage and then through a positive stage, and you have exactly what you photographed with your camera.

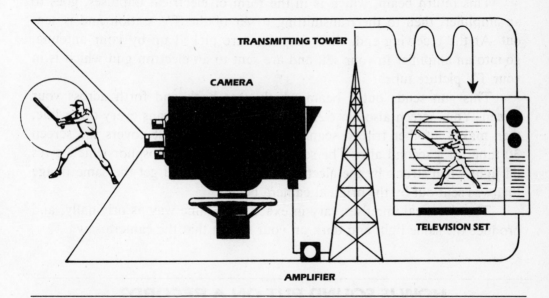

TRANSMITTING TOWER

CAMERA

TELEVISION SET

AMPLIFIER

HOW ARE TELEVISION PICTURES SENT AND RECEIVED?

"Television" really means "seeing at a distance." It is a method of sending pictures of events as they happen ("live"), or motion pictures from film, or "video tape" recordings. At the same time the pictures are broadcast, the sound is sent along by radio.

First we must understand that "pictures" are not sent through the air. What is transmitted are electrical impulses. This means that a picture has to be changed into electrical impulses at one end those electrical impulses changed back into a picture at the other end. Let's see, in basic terms, how this is done.

A camera lens focuses a picture on a light-sensitive plate of glass. This plate throws off electrons. In the bright areas of the picture, it throws off many electrons, and in the dark areas, few electrons. The electrons are collected on a target plate.

Now in this camera tube, at the other end from the target plate, there is an electron gun which throws a beam on the target plate. This beam is a "scanning" beam; it sweeps back and forth in 525 lines across the target plate so that it covers the entire surface 30 times in one second! The beam that bounces back is changed (modulated) according to whether it strikes a bright or dark area. The return beam is sometimes strong, sometimes weak, according to the image on the target plate.

This return beam, which is in the form of electrical impulses, goes to an amplifier, then to the transmitting tower of the TV station and is sent out. At the receiving end, these impulses are picked up by your antenna, go into an amplifier in your set, and are sent to an electron gun which is in your TV picture tube.

This gun sends out a beam which goes back and forth across your screen. Your screen also has 525 lines and the beam scans every other line, then makes another trip to scan the remaining lines. It covers the screen 30 times in a second also. The screen is coated with phosphor which gives off light when struck by the electron beam, and so you get the same image that was sent out by the original camera beam!

The electrical impulses vary in exactly the same way as originally, and produce the same light and dark on your screen that the camera saw.

HOW IS SOUND PUT ON A RECORD?

Today, with hi-fi, stereo, LP, and tape all available to reproduce sound in the home, we are certainly far from the simple phonograph that was invented by Thomas Edison. But the basic principles for capturing sound remain the same.

Sounds, whether speech or instrumental music, are caused by vibrations of air. To reproduce sounds, these vibrations must be "caught." Let us say the air vibrations are caught in the mouthpiece of a tube. At the other end of the tube there is a flexible disk and a cutting tool. As the vibrations come through the tube, the disk flutters, and the cutting tool moves with the disk.

At the same time, a plate of soft, waxy material revolves under the tool. There is a continuous groove on the surface of this plate that goes in a spiral from the outside edge to the center. The point of the tool is in the groove, and as it vibrates it marks the groove from side to side. In this way the vibrations are "caught."

Now suppose the cutting tool is removed and we put a needle in its place. As the record spins, the needle follows the markings in the groove. This makes the disk vibrate. The vibrating disk moves the air in the tube and produces the sounds that were caught!

Naturally, this is only the basic, simple principle of how a phonograph and records work. Modern recording methods are much more complicated. For example, sound waves can be converted to a series of electric currents. The fluctuating sound waves are made to produce a fluctuating electric current. This current is amplified. It then goes to a magnet to which a cutting tool is attached.

In picking up sound from the record, the needle presses on crystals in the pickup arm. The crystals set up an electric current that fluctuates with the vibrations of the needle. This current is amplified and it is made to push and pull the cone in the loudspeaker which sets up vibrations that we hear as sound.

HOW ARE TAPE RECORDINGS MADE?

Since the days back in 1877, when Thomas Edison made the first sound recording, so many great improvements have been made that it's almost impossible to keep up with them. Today especially, the whole science of sound recording and reproduction is moving ahead very rapidly, and all of us are enjoying the benefits of these advances.

Tape recording is one of the greatest developments in this field. What most people don't know is that it plays an important part in the making of records. In making records, the original sound is picked up by one or more microphones. It is recorded on a special kind of tape called "magnetic tape." What happens is that sound is changed into electrical signals which cause particles in the tape to be magnetized in a special way. When the tape is played, those magnetized particles give off the same electrical signals, which are then converted into sound.

Magnetic tape is used in making records because it can be edited. This means it can be cut apart and recombined, so that parts can be left out, new parts can be put in place of old, and so on.

The sound from the tape is fed to a disk cutter, which cuts grooves in a smooth lacquer disk. From this disk, master records are made, and these masters are later used to press records. Pressure and steam heat are used in the process of cutting the grooves in the soft record material.

This is how tape is used in making recordings, but as you know, the tape itself can be used as the final recording. The tape can be played without ever making a record. The development of this kind of tape was a long process. At first, spools of wire were used, and later, tape was made of solid metal. But the results were only fair.

When the Allies invaded Germany during World War II, they found that tape recorders of very good quality were being used in broadcasting stations. The secret was that tape made of plastic was being used. Once we found out how to use plastic for making tape recordings, many advances were quickly made.

Because the sound is put on tape by magnetizing particles on the surface of the tape, it can be played thousands of times without becoming noisy or losing its quality. It can be erased by being demagnetized, and then new sounds can be recorded on the same tape!

HOW ARE MIRRORS MADE?

For thousands of years, the only mirrors used by man were made of polished metal—brass, bronze, silver, or gold.

In about 1300, the craftsmen in Venice discovered a way of making mirrors of glass by backing them with a coating of mercury and tin. Very soon, these glass mirrors took the place of metal ones. But even these glass mirrors were far from perfect. In 1691, in France, a way of making plate glass was discovered. Because plate glass has more weight and brilliance, it is much more suited to mirrors than ordinary glass.

The next great step forward was the use of a thin silver coating on the back of a mirror instead of the tin-mercury mixture. Not only were the mercury fumes dangerous to the workmen, but the new silver coating reflected more rays of light and made better mirrors. It also led to speeding up the process of manufacturing and made mirrors less expensive.

Today, plate glass one-quarter inch in thickness is used in making the best-grade mirrors. The glass is first cut to the desired size with a diamond cutter. In the "roughing mill" the edges are treated with sand and water. It is next smoothed with fine sandstone and polished with rouge-covered felt buffers.

Before silvering, a thorough cleansing takes place to insure clearness. The glass is then placed on a warm, padded table. Over it is poured a mixture of ammonia, tartaric acid, and nitrate of silver. This readily sticks to the glass because of the heat. Then the silver is protected with a coat of shellac, and an application of paint which is free from oils and acids that would injure the silver.

Today, of course, mirrors have many more uses than merely to see one's self. Rear vision mirrors in automobiles are important to safe driving. Long-handled little mirrors are used by dentists to let them look into hard-to-see places. Mirrors are a vital part of the periscopes of submarines. The image striking one mirror in a tube is sent down the tube to the other mirror into which the observer is looking.

Mirrors are also used in telescopes, in flashlights, in searchlights, in headlights of automobiles, and in lamps in lighthouses. In most of these, however, the curved reflector, or mirror, is usually of a highly polished metal that concentrates the light and throws it ahead.

HOW DO EYEGLASSES CORRECT VISION?

Just imagine what life was like for millions of people before eyeglasses were invented! If you were nearsighted and you looked up at night you couldn't see clouds or distant mountains or birds flying through the air.

Today nearsighted people can see as much as people with normal eyes, because eyeglasses can correct their vision. To begin very simply, light enters our eye and falls on the retina in the eye, which is like the sensitized plate of a camera. Obviously, if the light falls in back of the retina or in front of it, we won't be able to see. So the eye has a lens to focus the light and make it fall in the right place.

When normal eyes look at distant objects, the image falls on the retina without any problem. But when the same eye looks at a close object (say less than 18 feet away), the image falls behind the retina. So the lens of the eye "accommodates," which means that a certain muscle contracts and

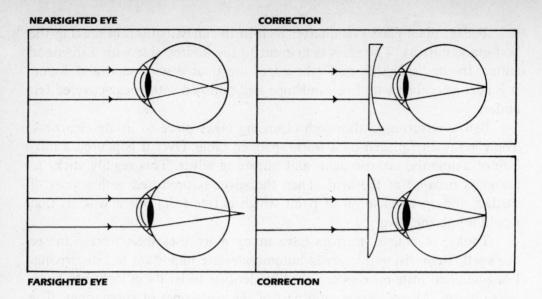

changes the shape of the lens. This makes the image fall on the retina and the eye sees the object clearly.

Now, two things can happen to make this accommodation impossible naturally. First, as people get older the lenses in the eyes lose their elasticity. They can't change shape to focus images correctly. The second thing is that some people are born with eyes that are too short or too long.

People with too short eyes are farsighted. They can see distant objects well, but they must accommodate very strongly to see near objects. Sometimes it is impossible to do this enough to focus the image on the retina. So they wear glasses. The glasses do the job that their own eye lenses cannot do. They focus the image on the retina and don't have to accommodate at all.

A nearsighted person has eyes that are too long. The image is focused in front of the retina and looks blurred. But the nearsighted person can do nothing about it. If he accommodates (makes the muscle contract the eye), it will only make the image move farther forward. So he wears glasses that focus the image farther back and on the retina, and then he can see clearly.

WHAT IS A CULTURED PEARL?

About 4,000 years ago, a Chinese fisherman who decided that oysters might satisfy his hunger opened a few and was probably the first man to discover pearls!

What are pearls and how are they produced? Pearls are made of the same material as the mother-of-pearl lining in the shell of the oyster. The body of the oyster is very tender, so to protect itself the oyster secretes this mother-of-pearl lining to provide a smooth surface against its body.

When an irritating object, such as a grain of sand, manages to get inside the oyster's shell, the oyster coats it with layer after layer of mother-of-pearl—and this becomes a pearl!

When this happens naturally, the pearl may be perfectly shaped. But man has found a way to help the oyster along in the making of pearls. A bit of sand or a tiny piece of mother-of-pearl is inserted between the shell and the outer skin of the oyster. After two or three years, when these shells are taken from the water and opened, a pearl is found inside. These are called "cultured" pearls, and are usually not perfectly shaped.

In Japan, they have now learned how to make even cultured pearls perfect! The irritating material is put right into the body of the oyster. This is really a surgical operation requiring great care and delicacy, because the oyster must be kept alive. But it's an operation well worth performing!

Pearl divers, almost naked and wearing nose clips, go down by means of a rope about 80 feet and stay under water about a minute at a time. They scoop up all the shells they can and put them into floating tubs. In some parts of the world, of course, pearl divers now have all kinds of modern diving equipment and stay down for hours at a time.

The largest pearl ever found is said to have been two inches long and four inches around! Because real pearls are so expensive, most of us buy artificial pearls. The French make beautiful artificial pearls by taking hollow glass beads and lining them with a substance that comes from the shiny scales of certain fish, then filling the beads with wax. These "pearls" can hardly be told apart from the real thing!

WHAT IS PLASTIC?

The word plastic means "capable of being molded or modeled." When heated, plastics are somewhat like modeling clay. They can be molded into shapes which last when the material is cooled. This is what gives them their name.

There is no need to go into a description of the many uses to which plastics have been put. Probably not a day goes by in our life in which we don't use or touch a plastic product.

But what is a plastic? The starting point in making a plastic is the molecule. It is the smallest division of matter that still acts like the whole material from which it comes.

The chemist causes the molecules of certain materials to form a long chain, the links being the molecules. The new "long-chain" molecule acts differently from the single molecule. It creates materials with new properties. When molecules link into chains we say they "polymerize."

Sometimes two different types of molecules are joined to form materials called "copolymers." A chain of two types of molecules acts differently from long chains made up of either type alone. So you see, the chemist can constantly create new materials, or plastics, to suit his needs.

A "polymer," or material made of long-chain molecules, is the beginning of a plastic. It has to be changed to be suitable for molding. It is ground into fine powder or made into pellets. To this, colors are added, and chemicals are worked in to make it flexible. Sometimes plasticizers are added. These are chemicals which change a plastic that is stiff as a blackboard into a material flexible enough for a raincoat.

Plastics have many special properties which make them very useful for special purposes. They resist the flow of electricity, they insulate against heat, they are light in weight and wear well, and they can be made unbreakable.

Each kind of plastic is derived from different materials. Some may come from coal, some from salt, some from wood or cotton fibers, etc. But in each case the molecules have to be rearranged in the right way and chemicals must be added to produce the desired plastic.

WHAT IS NYLON?

The first fiber ever made entirely by man is nylon, which was announced to the world in 1938.

It was created as the result of some experiments being conducted to find out why certain molecules join together to make "giant" molecules, such as are found in rubber and cotton.

One day, a material was produced that stretched like warm taffy candy. When it cooled, it could be stretched even farther, and as it was stretched it became elastic and stronger. This made the chemists working on the experiment wonder whether this new material could be used to create a textile fiber. They decided to try, and after eight long years of work they announced the new fiber known as nylon.

Nylon is made from four common elements: carbon, hydrogen, nitrogen, and oxygen. These elements are all found in nature. For instance, carbon is found in coal, nitrogen and oxygen in air, and hydrogen in water. Actually, in the making of nylon the basic materials are obtained from natural gas, petroleum, oat hulls, and corn cobs!

Nylon is formed by hooking two different kinds of molecules together to form larger molecules. When these two molecules join together, they form a material called "nylon salt."

When nylon salt is heated in a big pressure cooker, the molecules of the salt hook together and form the long chain of molecules called "a polymer." The polymer becomes a thick liquid when it is heated. This liquid is forced through a disk with tiny holes and it comes out as fibers which become hard as they are cooled. Then these tiny fragments of fibers are gathered together into a single yarn.

After stretching this yarn three or four times its original length, it becomes strong and elastic and we have nylon!

WHAT IS WOOL?

One of the first fibers man ever used for making cloth is wool. The use of wool began so long ago, in fact, that we don't know its beginning. The ancient Greeks spun and wove wool, and they learned how to do it from the Egyptians!

Wool is a kind of hair which grows on sheep and many other animals. The surface of all hair is covered with tiny scales, so small that we can only see them with a powerful microscope. These scales overlap, like the shingles on a roof. In a hair, the scales lie down flat, but in wool the edges stick out, and the natural "crimp" in wool helps make it useful as a fiber for cloth.

There are various grades of wool, depending on the sheep from which it comes. There is an interesting story in connection with this. For hundreds of years, the finest wool was produced in Spain from a kind of sheep called "the merino." When the Spanish Armada was sunk years ago, some of the ships went down off the north coast of Scotland. But a few merino sheep were washed ashore alive. These were bred with the native mountain sheep of Scotland, and from this came the famous Cheviot breed of sheep, which is one of the finest producers of wool in Great Britain.

Wool can be obtained from other animals than sheep. Angora and cashmere goats produce wool, as do the camel, alpaca, llama, and vicuña. A single sheep may yield as much as eight pounds of fleece, which is the name for this hair. But as much as half of this is dirt, grease, and a substance called "the yolk" of the wool. All of this has to be removed by a process called "scouring" before the wool can be used.

After the wool is sorted into various grades, scoured, and dried, it goes through a whole series of steps that includes dyeing, carding, and combing. Then it is spun into yarn and finally it's ready to be woven into cloth.

The first successful woolen mill in the United States was set up at Newberry, Massachusetts, in 1790. But American wool has never really been considered to be of the highest quality, so a third of all the wool used in this country is imported!

HOW ARE BLACKBOARDS MADE?

What would school be like if we didn't have blackboards? Think of the hundreds and hundreds of hours we spend during our school years either writing on the blackboard or reading what the teacher has written on it. What is that blackboard really made of?

Of course, many people know it's made of a substance called "slate." But what is slate? Interestingly enough, slate is a material that is millions and millions of years old. It all began when tiny particles of clay gradually sifted down to the bottoms of lakes and seas millions of years ago.

As they lay there at the bottom of the sea, they slowly formed a soft mud. As time went on, this mud hardened and became a kind of mud-rock called "shale." The earth was still going through violent changes, and at one time the crust heaved upward in that part where the shale was. The layers of shale were folded up into wrinkles. The other rocks squeezed and flattened the shale so hard that it became slate.

Because the original clay particles that made up the slate were deposited in layers at the bottom of the sea, the slate that finally developed has layers, too. This is one of the reasons slate is so useful for so many purposes. It not only makes blackboards, but is also used for roofs of buildings, sinks, drainboards, and a great number of other articles.

Slate is taken from quarries or from underground mines in big blocks, which are divided into smaller blocks, before they are removed to be split.

In making a piece of slate, the splitter takes blocks about 3 inches thick. He holds a chisel in a certain position against the edge of the block, and taps it lightly with a mallet. A crack appears, and by using the chisel the block is split into two pieces with smooth and even surfaces.

The splitter keeps on repeating this process until he has changed the original block into about 16 or 18 separate "slates." In the case of a roofing tile, the slate is split until it's about one-sixth of an inch thick.

Slate comes in many colors—black, blue, purple, red, green, or gray—depending on the presence of various materials in the original clay deposits. Black slate is the result of living materials that turned to carbon in the original muds.

HOW ARE CRAYONS MADE?

On the surface of the ocean there live many forms of very tiny plants and animals. Among these are certain one-celled animals called "Foraminifera," which have shells of lime.

When these animals die, their tiny shells sink to the ocean floor, and in time they form a thick layer there. This layer becomes cemented and compressed into a soft limestone called "chalk."

Men have used this soft limestone for hundreds of years, and one of these uses has been to make crayon. In fact, one form of this chalk called "red earth" has been used to make crayons since ancient times.

Today, many crayons are also made from artificially prepared mixtures. This consists of a base of certain types of clay, to which a variety of pigments are added. The material is then "cemented" together by the use of an adhesive. By adding varying amounts of coloring matter to a given quantity of the base, any shade of tint can be obtained.

You may think of crayons as something that children use for their drawings. But actually, chalk and crayons have had an important role in the history of art.

At the beginning of the 16th century, the artists used chiefly black chalk on white paper. But later on, they began to use it with other mediums to suggest color First they used black chalk with a little white on a tinted paper. Then they began to use black and red crayon, heightened with white, on various shades of paper.

Finally, the great French artist Watteau began to use red crayon in such marvelous ways that he opened up a whole new field of art.

If you are interested in drawing, and haven't yet begun to use oil paints, you should be encouraged by the examples of some of the world's greatest artists. Holbein, Van Dyck, Titian, and Tintoretto created masterpieces with chalk and crayon. Michelangelo, Raphael, and Leonardo da Vinci also used chalk and crayon to create works of lasting beauty!

WHAT IS GLUE?

The word "glue" comes from Old French and Late Latin verbs meaning "to draw together." The idea of using a substance to hold things together is a very old one. On the walls of an Egyptian tomb more than 3,000 years old, there is a painting showing workmen using glue!

Since the meaning of "glue" is "that which sticks together," many substances are called "glue." For example, there are mineral glues, vegetable glues, marine glues, and many synthetic glues.

But the traditional glue is made from bones, sinews, and the hides of animals. These are properly prepared, heated, and then the solution is dried. In fact, if you've ever taken out a cooked chicken which has been put in the refrigerator, you've seen a jelly on top of the liquid. This is really an impure glue solution.

When glue is prepared commercially, the hot solutions are filtered, clarified, and evaporated. The concentrate is then dried. Another method used in preparing glue is to allow the solutions to chill to a firm jelly. The jelly is then cut into thin slices which are spread on nets. The nets are then dried in currents of warm air in a drying tunnel.

Glue is used in small quantities in hundreds of ways in many industries. For example, wood joints and veneers in furniture, pianos, and toys require glue. It is very important in bookbinding and the making of paper boxes. Gummed paper of all kinds has glue, and so do fireworks, match heads, and dolls' heads!

When you have new paper money and hear it "crackle," it's because the paper has been sized with glue. Sandpaper couldn't be made without glue to hold down the grains.

Glue, being made of natural substances, decays quickly, so preservatives are added. But despite this, if you have a solution of glue standing around, it is likely to mold or rot, and develop a vile odor. That's why glue should be freshly prepared. This means making a solution out of the granulated form, in which form glue is usually sold in bulk.

WHAT MAKES A BASEBALL CURVE?

Everybody who loves and follows baseball knows that a pitcher can make a ball curve. But strangely enough, there have been some attempts to prove that a baseball doesn't really curve! This has been done with a camera, and the idea was that the curve is an optical illusion.

Luckily for all the great pitchers who earn so much money because of their ability to throw a good curve ball, it has been demonstrated that a baseball can be made to curve as much as 6½ inches from its normal path.

The explanation of what makes a baseball curve is tied up with a rather complicated scientific law or "effect." This was discovered by a man called Bernoulli, and is known as "the Bernoulli effect."

Bernoulli pointed out that there are two kinds of pressure in a fluid, such as air or water. One is static, one is dynamic. The dynamic pressure is created when a moving fluid (such as air) comes into contact with an object. Static pressure is the pressure existing within the fluid itself, the pressure of one atom against another. The Bernoulli effect states that the static pressure goes down as the speed goes up.

Now we're ready for the baseball. When the pitcher wants to throw a curve, he makes the ball spin as it leaves his hand. As the ball spins, it carries air around with it by friction. On one side of the spinning ball, this air moves with the current of air caused by the forward motion of the ball. In other words, the air passing the ball and the air spinning around the ball are going in the same direction on one side. On the other side, the air spinning around the ball is going in the opposite direction to the motion of the air past the ball.

The result is, the air speed is greater on one side of the ball than on the other. Now remember, we said greater speed makes the static pressure go down. So the ball moves toward the side where there is lower static pressure and it "curves"!

WHAT MAKES A BOOMERANG RETURN?

One of the oldest and most peculiar weapons ever developed by man is the boomerang. The word "boomerang," by the way, comes from a single tribe in New South Wales, who called it that long ago.

Although the boomerang is hardly more than a curved club, it puzzled science for many years. Nobody seemed able to explain why it behaved as it did in the air. It is used by savage tribes in Australia, northeast Africa, and southern India, and by the Hopi Indians of Arizona.

There are two kinds of boomerangs: the return and the nonreturn. The nonreturn boomerang is the heavier, and nearly straight. It is more deadly as a weapon than the return boomerang. It is said that a native can throw it and cut a small animal almost in two with it.

The return boomerang is better known to the world. But the natives of Australia consider it chiefly a toy, not a serious weapon. It may sometimes be used for killing birds.

It is made of hard wood and is curved at an angle of between 90 degrees and 120 degrees. One side is flat and the other is rounded. The arms are very slightly twisted in opposite directions, so that they are about 2 degrees off a plane drawn through the center of the boomerang. It is the pressure of the air on the bulge of the rounded side, together with the twist given it when thrown, which makes the boomerang circle and return.

The wild bushmen of Australia can make a boomerang curve in an amazing manner. They can throw it so that it will travel straight for 30 yards, describe a circle 50 yards in diameter, and then return to the thrower. Or they can make it hit the ground, circle in the air, and return.

A boomerang is thrown forward with a downward twist of the wrist. Boomerangs have been known to travel as far as 400 feet before returning.

HOW ARE FIREWORKS MADE?

Fireworks are so old that nobody knows who first made them, or when! The credit for inventing "pyrotechny" (the art of making fireworks) is usually given to the Chinese, because they had them hundreds of years before they were known in Europe.

Did you know that the ancient Greeks and Romans had fireworks of some sort? However, fireworks as we know them weren't really made until after gunpowder came into use and the science of chemistry had developed.

The basic materials used in making fireworks are saltpeter, sulphur, and charcoal. These ingredients are ground together into a fine powder. Then, in order to obtain the various spectacular effects that make us say "Oooh!" and "Ahhh!," other things are added, such as nitrates of lead, barium, and aluminum.

The colors in fireworks, which add so much to their beauty and effect, are obtained by adding various salts of metals: strontium for red; barium for green; sodium for yellow; copper for blue. By using iron filings, showers of dazzling sparks can be obtained.

A simple Roman candle is made by stopping the bottom of a cardboard tube with clay or plaster and placing above this a layer of gunpowder. Next comes a hard "ball" of a powder designed to burn but not explode. Around this is a layer of "inflammant," which means a substance that bursts into flame.

Then there is a thicker layer of slow-burning powder called "fuze," another of gunpowder, above this a second "ball" with its inflammant, and so on. When the tube is filled, an igniting fuse sticks out of the paper cup which covers the mouth of the tube.

When this is lighted, it ignites the top layer of slow-burning powder, which gradually burns down to the inflammant surrounding the topmost ball. Then the ball itself catches fire, the gunpowder explodes, and this drives the glowing ball from the tube. This is repeated until all the balls are expelled. So you can see there really is an "art" to making fireworks!

HOW IS CHOCOLATE MADE?

Long before chocolate was made in solid pieces, it was enjoyed as a drink. The Aztecs made it by boiling the crushed beans of the cacao tree with water and serving it cold, highly spiced, and seasoned with pepper!

Spanish explorers, who discovered this drink among the Aztecs, didn't like peppers. So they invented a new recipe by adding an equal amount of sugar to the cacao before boiling it. The Spaniards kept the secret of their new drink for about 100 years! Finally, in the middle of the 17th century, a Frenchman discovered how to make the finely ground cacao beans into cakes of chocolate.

Cacao beans are gathered in this way. Skilled workmen cut ripe pods from the cacao tree. After being cut, the pods are split open and the pulp scooped out. This is allowed to ferment for several days. Then the mass is dried in the sun and the seeds are separated and bagged for shipment to market.

Upon arrival at the chocolate manufacturer's mill, the beans are first cleaned to remove any foreign material, and then roasted. As they roast, their husks are loosened, and in another operation the husks are blown away, and the inner kernel is broken into bits called "nibs."

For chocolate, the nibs are ground under heavy stone mills. The oil within them turns the mass into a thick substance called "chocolate liquor." This, when hard, is the bitter chocolate used in candymaking and baking.

Sweet chocolate is the same product combined with sugar and other substances. In making cocoa, part of the fat is separated after the nibs are ground. This fat, called "cocoa butter," is used for cosmetics and medicines, and forms an ingredient in the manufacture of sweet chocolate. What remains is ground fine to make cocoa.

INDEX